"The Beauty of a Doctoral Degree"

Crowned with a Doctorate: Stories of Women Who Rose

Dr. Marquita A. Taylor

"I can do all things through Christ who strengthens me."

Philippians 4:13

A note from Dr. Marquita A. Taylor

There is a sacred beauty in a woman's rise, especially when she dares to pursue knowledge at the highest levels, often while juggling full lives, full hearts, and full calendars. This book, The Beauty of a Doctoral Degree, Crowned with a Doctorate: Stories of Women Who Rose, is a celebration of that rise. It is a chorus of voices, each woman telling the truth of her journey; brilliant, bruising, bold, and showing what it means to wear the crown of doctor not just in title, but in testimony. There is something regal about a woman who refuses to dim her light, who dares to learn, to lead, to labor in spaces never designed with her in mind. This book is not just about academic achievement. It is about the sacred becoming. The quiet revolutions. The fire-forged grace of women who chose the long road to elevation, and emerged not just credentialed, but crowned. We are taught to revere titles like "Doctor," to associate them with authority and excellence. But for the women in these pages, the title is more than that. It is proof. Proof that brilliance can wear braids and bilingual tongues. That intellect can be wrapped in mothering, mourning, and making a way out of no way, that a doctoral degree can be both armor and altar. These stories are not sanitized. They are not softened for comfort. They are raw, radiant, and real. Each one carries the weight of nights spent questioning, rewriting, and starting over. Of being the only one. Of being overlooked, underestimated, and still standing. Each woman here has walked through fire, and rather than being burned, she built.I envisioned this book not as a compilation of academic resumes, but as a mirror. A mirror that reflects the depth of discipline, the moments of doubt, the rituals of resilience, and the grace we gathered along the way. These stories are not only about achievement—they are about transformation. Each woman featured here did more than defend a dissertation; she defended her dreams. She battled imposter syndrome, quieted internalized doubt, and often walked paths where there were few footprints before her.

This is a book for every woman who has ever wondered if she was smart enough, strong enough, worthy enough to dream bigger. It is for the girl who grew up speaking softly and now teaches with thunder in her voice. It is for the mother writing her dissertation with a baby on her hip. It is for the daughter of immigrants, of the South, of the struggle, who now puts "Dr." in front of her name and knows it was never just for her, but for everyone who poured into her.

Why "crowned?" Because the doctorate, while earned through rigorous labor, is more than a degree, it is a visible mark of an invisible triumph. It signifies not only intellect, but identity, intention, and immense inner power. To be "crowned" is to be seen, to be recognized, and to embrace the majesty of one's journey.

The Beauty of a Doctoral Degree is a declaration. A celebration. A testimony of what happens when women reclaim scholarship as a form of self-love, resistance, and legacy. It is a love letter to every woman who dared to go further, not just for a degree, but for her destiny.

To the women who grace these pages with their stories: I honor you. Your voice matters, your story matters, and you are, without question, beautifully crowned.

To the readers who hold this book in your hands: may you see what's possible. May you feel the fire. And may you know, without question, that you too are worthy of the crown.

With love, power, reverence, and solidarity,

Marquita

Table of Contents

CHAPTER 1

DR. BREONNA STONE

I grew up in Milwaukee, Wisconsin, which is a city marked by its deep-seated segregation and historical disinvestment in communities like mine. Atkinson, the exact neighborhood I called home, was one of the places people often prayed to leave. But for me, it became a paradox: a space of pain and purpose. It was in this community, nestled between broken sidewalks and blaring sirens, that I began to understand what it meant to live with faith, resilience, and a quiet fire that would eventually push me forward. Later in life, I'd learn how my community got to what I knew it was. As a child, however, I feared it and wanted desperately to move my family as far away from it as possible.

Home, Hope, and Holy Ground

My parents were the very picture of working-class strength. My mother, a Child Care Supervisor, and my father, a self-taught Chemist, made the most with what we had. They sacrificed to give my brother and me an abundance of opportunities, and most importantly, love. Our home was clean, warm, and rooted in faith. We didn't have everything, but we never went without. My brother and I truly grew up with more than most.

My father was calm in every storm. I remember waking up from nightmares and running into my parents' room. Without fail, he would grab his Bible and gently read scripture to comfort me. He'd stay up as long as I needed him to review scripture and Bible stories, reminding me that I was a child of God and did not have to fear anything. Those words weren't just biblical promises; they became the emotional blanket that wrapped around me night after night.

Fear and Foundations

Despite my parents' love and our home being a refuge, the world outside brought on a lot of anxiety for me. I witnessed things I should never have seen. Violence, abuse, and drug activity were common occurrences despite how hard my parents worked to keep us sheltered from it. I was always a very inquisitive child, so often I'd lie awake in my bed, and even though I should have been asleep, I wanted to look out of my window and see what was going on. I've seen men dragging women down the street, drug exchanges, and people who appeared to be out of their minds on either a substance or mentally. I can recall how one night a bullet tore through the walls of my bedroom while I slept. The next day, police entered our home and confirmed what I already sensed: someone had been killed directly across the street. On another occasion, my mother, brother, and I were chased in our car by a man wielding a gun who was clearly drunk or high. He got behind us as we left our home, driving erratically as though he was high on something or had lost his mind. I remember my mom driving as fast as she could to get us to safety while offering my brother and me comfort during the situation. To this day, I think about this experience and how we could have lost our lives in an instant. Fear became my constant companion, but it also became my motivator. I decided early on that I didn't just want to leave my community and never look back. My childhood home, while a place of fear, became the foundation for my purpose.

The Gift of Exposure

My parents made it their mission to ensure I had every opportunity to grow beyond our community. I was enrolled in a variety of activities, including ballet, tennis, soccer, summer programs, and swimming; you name it. They exposed me to possibilities outside our neighborhood, allowing me to build my network in Milwaukee at a very young age and also afforded me more opportunities, from scholarships to traveling. I began to see what life could be like with hard work, discipline, education, and resilience. I also began to notice the differences between where I lived and where I visited.

When I started college, I couldn't help but notice the huge differences between the campus neighborhood and where I grew up. My classmates strolled the streets with ease, some jogging with their headphones in, as if they had nothing to worry about. The area around the university felt clean, safe, and well-maintained. That shocked me because it was only a few miles from Atkinson. Back home, liquor stores were on every corner, houses looked run-down, and walking around without paying attention just wasn't smart. The contrast was hard to ignore. The dissonance was jarring. It left me with questions about why things were the way they were and why it seemed that some communities were allowed to thrive while others were left behind.

Finding Language, Finding Self

It wasn't until I got to the University of Wisconsin-Milwaukee that I began to find language for what I had been experiencing. Through my Africology courses, I began to understand redlining, systemic racism, and the intentional policies that created neighborhoods like mine. I learned that the differences I saw weren't accidental; they were designed. The rundown buildings, liquor stores, and lack of grocery stores or safe parks were the result of policies that determined which neighborhoods deserved investment and which didn't. One stat that stayed with me is that Milwaukee was ranked the most segregated city in the U.S. as recently as 2020. It gave language to what I had felt my whole life, but couldn't put into words. As Audre Lorde once said, "There is no such thing as a single-issue struggle because we do not live single-issue lives." For me, it wasn't just about poverty or fear of my own people; it was about race, access, power, and being deliberately left out. I realized I had misplaced my frustration for far too long and that my community wasn't the problem. Systems were!

As bell hooks once wrote, "There is no transformation of life without the embrace of pain." That's exactly what learning to name these structures did for me. I began to see that the pain my people were carrying and the pain that came with growing up in fear of my community had a purpose. It lit a fire that would fuel my academic, spiritual, and professional journey.

Mary B's Prophecy

Long before I ever understood what "the academy" even meant, my granny, Mary Charles Booker, saw something in me that I hadn't yet seen in myself. We'd sit together on the couch, tucked under a blanket, watching Oprah reruns while she snuck me little sips of coffee, smiling like we had a secret. She'd look at me with this calm certainty and say, "You're going to be a Doctor one day, Bre. Get all the education you can." To her, education wasn't just about books or degrees; it was a key. It was freedom and security. A passport. She'd tell me that with enough of it, there'd be no place I couldn't go, no room I couldn't enter.

She'd talk to me about Oprah's work in Africa, about the school she built for girls, and how education could change the world. Those conversations cracked open something in me. They made me believe that I didn't have to be limited by where I came from or what I saw outside my bedroom windows. Now, let's be clear, this was the same woman who'd march outside with a towel in hand if I was sitting on the porch with my legs gapped, reminding me, "A lady crosses her legs." My granny was both soft and firm at the same time. She was always teaching me and always shaping my mind, whether I embraced it at the time or not.

As I got older, I realized Granny wasn't just talking to me; she was preparing me. Speaking purpose over me before I had the words to claim it. She was planting seeds of substance, grace, and vision, long before I knew I'd need them. Looking back now, I realize my journey didn't start with college or even high school. It began on that couch, coffee in hand, listening to a woman who already knew what I was becoming. Her words stuck. Even after dementia dimmed her memory, I held on to that vision she cast over my life. And while I never did buy her that Punch Buggie she wanted me to drive her around in, her faith in me became a driving force.

The Decision to Pursue a PhD

After completing my master's degree, I was exhausted but not done. I knew I owed it to myself and to Granny to keep going. I applied for a doctoral program at the same University and found myself in an interview with an older white man. At first, I answered his questions with polished, rehearsed responses. It wasn't that I was ashamed of where I came from and what my "why" was; I didn't believe he really wanted to hear it and felt that this exchange was meant to ensure I was like my peers. I believed he was merely checking a box and that if I stayed within those expectations, I'd surely land the opportunity. Halfway through the interview, I stopped. I took a deep breath and spoke my truth about growing up on Atkinson, witnessing violence, and wanting to focus my research on Black people in the name of representation. I told that man that I had a lot of people who needed to see me earn this degree! I assured him that I didn't plan to stop at earning my PhD and that I wanted to publish research that would lend to the empowerment of disenfranchised groups like the one I was an insider to. Did I mention I told him about my praying grandmother who'd passed away just before I completed my bachelor's degree and how I made a promise I'd intended to keep. When I finished, with a big smile on his face, he thanked me. "Our program will be better because of you," he said. That was my unofficial acceptance.

Imposter Syndrome and Over-Celebration

The doctoral journey was far from smooth. I was the youngest in my cohort and one of the few Black women in the group. At first, I was praised excessively for my class contributions. But over time, I began to feel like a spectacle. Was I being celebrated or tokenized? I'll come back to this a little later.

My first summer seminar hit me like a wave; part exciting, part overwhelming. I was the youngest in my intergenerational group by far, and one of only a few Black women. Right away, the questions came fast and blunt from my white peers: "Why a doctorate?" "Why now?" "Do you have kids?" Several of my peers told me I was just a baby, that they hadn't even considered a PhD at my age. They didn't mean to be hurtful, but their words stuck with me. I remember after the first night of the summer seminar, I went to my best friend's dorm and cried. I called my friends. I called my family. And every single one of them reminded me: You belong there. You're not there by mistake. You didn't get in by accident. That was the first time I started questioning whether I had moved too fast or whether I really had what it took to be in this space.

Once the actual coursework began, things became even more challenging. My study group was comprised of people from Milwaukee, which felt familiar, but something still felt off. I started noticing a pattern. Whenever I spoke in class, even when I was just sharing a simple thought, I'd get a round of applause or over-the-top praise. But if someone else said the same thing, the class was silent or simply not as celebratory. At first, I thought it was encouragement. But over time, it started to feel like I was being watched more than celebrated. It made me wonder, do they actually see me, or just the idea of me? Had I unknowingly become the token Black girl in the room? Was the support authentic?

That tension stayed with me. I found myself shrinking a little in class, hoping not to draw too much attention to myself. I'd sit in the back, scrolling through things that had nothing to do with our discussion. I began to feel distant from my classmates and even from the excitement I once had about being in the program. Imposter syndrome crept in, and it was loud. I started telling myself that I'd only gotten as far as I had academically because people liked me. I started to feel like a fraud, as if people would soon figure me out. It took deep conversations with my people, my mentor, my friends, and my tribe to pull me out of that fog. I had to go back to my foundation when these feelings really started to weigh in. I remembered my Granny's words. I leaned on scripture—Isaiah 41:10: "So do not fear, for I am with you; do not be dismayed, for I am your God. I will strengthen you and help you; I will uphold you with my righteous right hand." God hadn't brought me this far to leave me.

My first dissertation topic? Way too ambitious. I had printed more than 50 scholarly articles, ready to tackle the world. I should note that I began writing my dissertation during my second year of doctoral studies. My advisor gently encouraged me to narrow it down, to pick a more manageable path. I tried, but I could feel myself getting overwhelmed. I didn't want to be in this program forever, but my original topic was near and dear to not just me but my community and my family. My original study would enable me to examine Aces scores among youth with incarcerated parents. I wanted to understand their life outcomes and conduct a 3-year study where I followed a sample of children who had incarcerated parents/guardians.

I wanted to finish and finish well, but the topic was so heavy. The more I learned, the more I realized that this topic would take more than three years to complete. One day, after praying and talking with my Chair, I decided I needed to change my topic. That's when my advisor shared a simple line that changed everything for me: "A good dissertation is a done dissertation."

Around that time, I started getting messages from Black women—some I knew well, others I barely knew at all. They reached out to cheer me on, to say they were proud, but in the same breath, they'd tear themselves down. "You're amazing," they'd say. "I could never do what you're doing. I'm not smart enough. I wouldn't even know where to begin." And every time I heard it, my heart sank. I never wanted my shine to make another woman feel small. Their compliments felt heavy because behind them was pain, fear, and self-doubt. I didn't want to be put on a pedestal while they questioned their own worth. I wanted to say, "Sis, this win is yours too. There's room for all of us.

Many of them also assumed I had always loved school, that I had straight A's, or that I had some kind of secret sauce they didn't have. A few even told me they thought PhDs were for white people and were proud to see that I was "the" exception. Were they proud of me? Absolutely. But could they see themselves in the same space? Not yet. I dove into research about impostor syndrome, intersectionality, and feminist theory. I found bell hooks, and her words gave me life. One quote stuck with me and became my anchor: "I will not have my life narrowed down. I will not bow down to somebody else's whim or someone else's ignorance." I stopped playing small. I decided to center Black women in my research because our stories needed to be told, and because we deserved to be seen, not as tokens, but as scholars.

With my Chair and mentor's support, I scrapped my original topic and started fresh. I filled my desk with articles, drafts, and sticky notes. And just when I thought I was finding my rhythm, some of the same peers who once cheered me on began to question the value of my work. "Why only study Black women?" they asked. "Is this even scholarly research?" One guy flat out told me during a peer review session, "This isn't worthy of academic study." He couldn't see the worth. He didn't think it mattered. And he told me to consider choosing something "more relevant." This was the same man who thought my research on Black children with incarcerated parents/guardians was breathtaking.

He looked at me like I had three heads when I said I wanted to center Black women in my research. He was genuinely confused, like he couldn't understand why that would even matter. But the irony is, Malcolm X said it plain and clear: "The most disrespected person in America is the Black woman. The most unprotected person in America is the Black woman. The most neglected person in America is the Black woman." And that was decades ago, yet here I was, in a doctoral program, surrounded by people who still couldn't see our value. My classmates didn't get it because Black women are still too often overlooked, erased, or seen as an afterthought in academic spaces. But I refused to let us be forgotten in mine.

It stung. But it didn't stop me.

I wrote Chapter One of my dissertation, and after receiving numerous feedback, edits, and reviews, I managed to get it approved. I then wrote chapter two, which was extremely challenging. I couldn't quite wrap my mind around the theoretical framework. I watched numerous YouTube videos that guided me through setting up this chapter, and I still struggled. I tried talking to my peers, but their jargon went right over my head. I spent many hours in the library and student union, sitting with my theoretical framework, when one evening it finally clicked. It took reading a similar research study to consider the angle from which I wanted to create my own. I shared it with my chair and mentor, and both supported it. I then began writing, and after further revisions and edits, I was finally approved to move forward with the IRB. I decided to keep my sample small. I reached out to women who had experienced impostor syndrome and completed their terminal degrees.

I intentionally wanted to talk to Black women who had navigated these rigorous programs because I felt there was a lot to learn from them to encourage and inspire other Black women to take up space. I interviewed these women at their workplaces, in their homes, and virtually. I wanted to make the process as less daunting for them as possible. Every one of my participants allowed themselves to be vulnerable, open, and honest.

Writing was a never-ending process of receiving feedback, editing, and writing. I'd think I produced something solid and allowed myself to believe that my edits would stick; and my chair would send me write back to write some more. I had to trust this process as a part of the journey. Once I started sharing my work with my committee, I also began to receive feedback. My mentor was one of my committee members and a faculty member at the school with whom I had no prior relationship. None of them cut me any slack. I was writing and editing ad nauseam and then some more. I remember having to throw out whole pages and paragraphs and start over. At one point, I started making up a narrative in my head that my Chair simply didn't like me, which was so far from the truth. In my mind, he had it out for me. The whole time, I just needed to trust the process because he and my committee were, in fact, the individuals who would see me through the finish line.

They did just that!

I clung tightly to Dr. Marquita Taylor, my mentor throughout the entire process. She had walked the same path. She reminded me that just because people didn't understand my work didn't mean it wasn't valuable. When I hit a wall, she reminded me that resting wasn't quitting. She gave me space to be human. To be Black. To be brilliant. She never let me forget that I was enough.

Then came the curveball: my school announced it would be closing. On top of that, my dear uncle, Gerald White, was losing his battle with cancer. Everything felt like it was crumbling. I left my job to focus on finishing my dissertation, which brought new financial stress. I was tired, anxious, grieving, and overwhelmed. I told my friends, "Count me out of everything." I knew it was going to take everything in me to finish. I never doubted that God would make a way, but I knew that to finish strong, I had to have a level of discipline that I'd never had. I had to commit to this work because it was necessary.

While I left my full-time role to pursue my degree, I continued to teach part-time at my alma mater in a graduate program. It didn't pay much, but it gave me a sense of purpose. My students were parents, caregivers, and professionals. We were all tired, but we all had a degree to complete, and we encouraged each other to push forward. That space became a safe haven for both of us.

I worked nonstop writing, editing, and praying. I paid for an editor out of my pocket towards the end of my writing process. I stayed up late re-reading paragraphs, finding the right words. And finally, the day came after what felt like a million revisions. My defense. It was virtual, but I could feel the presence of everyone who mattered, from my mentor to my committee, my family, my students, and my ancestors. When they said,

"Congratulations, Dr. Stone," I cried. I had done the very thing I'd promised myself and my granny. I, the young girl from Atkinson, had kept my promise to my Granny, Mrs. Mary B. I had honored every part of the journey that brought me here. And I had done it my way, centering Black women so that they could be reminded that if I could do it, there was no limit to what they could do.

Mentorship, Marquita, and Moving Forward

Throughout all of this, Dr. Marquita Taylor never wavered in her sisterhood and mentorship to me. She was more than a mentor; she was a lifeline. When I felt overwhelmed, unsure, or on the brink of giving up, she reminded me of the promise I made to myself and the purpose behind my work. She didn't try to fix me or force me forward. Instead, she created space. She allowed me to be honest, to break down, to sit in the tension, and then reminded me, gently but firmly, of who I was. She did not allow me to throw pity parties for myself, and she offered hard truths.

Her presence in my life wasn't transactional or tied to titles. She walked alongside me, always showing up with wisdom, grace, and truth. In every conversation, she saw the fullness of me: the scholar, the daughter, the dreamer, the tired Black woman just trying to make it through one more draft. And she didn't just check in with a quick email; she carved out time, asked hard questions, stayed up reviewing my writing, and celebrated every single win, big or small.

I called her my "fave" for a reason. "Go 21, Go 21". The 21 Savage to my Drake! She was the gold standard for what mentorship should be. She helped me find my way back time and time again. If she believed in my work, I knew it was worthy. If she told me I had something important to say, I trusted her enough to keep writing. And long after the program ended, she's still here and still checking in, still showing up, still reminding me that I belong in every room I enter. Her mentorship was never just about helping me finish a degree; it was about preparing me to walk fully in my purpose. And for all of this, I am forever grateful.

Beyond the Degree

Today, I serve as the Interim Principal of a K-8 school in Milwaukee, the very city that shaped me. I've had the honor of watching two classes of eighth graders walk across the stage, their eyes full of hope, even if they don't yet know what's ahead. This year, I wore my doctoral regalia. I stood in front of them, not just as their principal, but as proof. I told them, "If I could do this, so can you." I had to remind them that I'm not some distant success story and still growing daily, but that I grew up in the same neighborhoods they're growing up in. I walked the same cracked sidewalks. I heard the same sirens at night. I told them that Milwaukee is still one of the most segregated cities in America, and that Black children here are far more likely to experience poverty, under-resourced schools, and trauma before they even hit their teens. I wasn't telling them anything they didn't already know, but their eyes were locked on me. I reminded them that they are more than a statistic and have everything in them to create a beautiful life for themselves. I told them and their families to keep God and prayer at the head of their lives, and how brilliantly they were each made.

Next month, I'll return to my role as Director of Operations. And while it's not lost on me that systems have long been used to harm and hold back entire communities like my own, I've personally grown to love them because I now see how powerful they can be when designed with intention, equity, and care. I love building structures in chaotic environments. But what I love most is showing up for Black and Brown children, not just in words, but in presence. I want them to see leadership that looks like them, loves them, and believes in them. And now, I'm preparing to release my first book, which is a love letter to Black women in academia. A survival guide and a testimony to remind them that they can do hard things. A reminder that we are not alone, and that our stories deserve to be told in our own words, on our own terms.

Take Up Space, Sis

To every Black woman reading this, I need you to hear me with your whole heart: you were never meant to shrink. You were made to take up space. You were born with purpose, brilliance, and a light that this world cannot dim. No matter where you come from, whether it's a neighborhood like mine or a place where you always felt like the only one in the room, you belong. Your presence matters. Your voice matters. Your dreams matter.

As Philippians 4:13 reminds us, "I can do all things through Christ who strengthens me." And that includes you, Sis. You can. You will. You are already doing more than you know. Bell hooks once said, "Living as we do in a white supremacist capitalist patriarchy, we are all socialized to internalize oppressive thinking." But here's the truth: you don't have to stay in that thinking. You get to unlearn it. You get to rise beyond it. And like Audre Lorde told us, "Caring for myself is not self-indulgence, it is self-preservation, and that is an act of political warfare." Your joy, your rest, your voice, and your resilience are all sacred. It's revolutionary.

Find your people. I pray that each of you gets to meet Dr. Marquita Taylor. Build a tribe that sees you, affirms you, and reminds you who you are. Guard your peace, as if your life depends on it, because sometimes it does. Pray without ceasing. Cry when it's heavy. But don't quit. You are not alone. We are many. We see you. And we're rising right alongside you. When I graduated with my doctoral degree, the percentage of black women PhD holders was 4.4%. It's our responsibility to increase that percentage and encourage one another along the way.

I would be remiss if I didn't also urge you to get clear about your why early on. While my grandmother prophesied over my life, I couldn't solely pursue a degree this rigorous on my own. I had to want it myself, and I had to remind myself that I was doing this for me! The process felt lonely, despite having my tribe and the support of others, on more occasions than not, due to the discipline, self-work, and level of consistency required to complete it. You will have days when you feel left out by your friends and family. You will lose friends who don't understand your vision and the sacrifices you must make in that season. You will miss birthdays, holidays, girls' trips, and other special occasions. All of those things will be there at the end of your degree. Trust me! Set your intentions and name your why. Write it down and make it clear! For me, I'd write sticky notes with my why and affirmations to put around my room, in my office, and even on my bathroom mirror, and they helped.

That said, once the intention and the why are set, go relentlessly towards your goal. When the road feels long, remember Isaiah 40:31: "But they that wait upon the Lord shall renew their strength; they shall mount up with wings as eagles; they shall run, and not be weary; and they shall walk, and not faint."

Keep going, Sis.

"

"To be Black. To be brilliant."

"Not only so, but we also glory in our sufferings, because we know that suffering produces perseverance; 4 perseverance, character; and character, hope."

Romans 5:3-4

CHAPTER 2

DR. LA TOYA S. GLENN

 I grew up as an only child to a dedicated military mother. Our life was filled with movement—new places, new people, new experiences. Traveling the world at a young age taught me resilience, adaptability, and the importance of service. Those early years shaped much of who I am today. Eventually, in my twenties, I decided to plant roots in Georgia, where I bought my first home and raised my three beautiful children.

As far back as I can remember, I wanted to be a doctor. As a child, I was sure I'd become a pediatrician. But once I entered college, a world of possibilities opened before me. I learned about the various types of doctors that exist beyond the medical field, and that's when I discovered industrial-organizational psychology. I found myself fascinated by the inner workings of business, leadership, and the psychological dynamics of the workplace. I realized that my true passion lay in developing organizations and creating environments where people could thrive.

Pursuing a terminal degree was never a question for me—it was a part of my life's blueprint. I have always considered myself a lifelong learner. Whether through an M.D., Ph.D., or any other pathway, I knew I was destined to reach the highest level of academic achievement. It wasn't just about a title; it was about legacy. I wanted to set an example for my children—one that showed them the power of perseverance, education, and purpose.

My journey to the doctorate took seven years. It was not an easy road. I was a full-time working mother, juggling responsibilities at home, at work, and in my studies. Distance learning became my path, offering the flexibility I needed to continue progressing toward my goal. It required discipline, structure, and effective time management. But I pushed through.

My children were my greatest motivation. They witnessed every stage of my doctoral process—the long nights, the moments of self-doubt, the celebrations. Whenever I felt weary or overwhelmed, I looked to them. They reminded me of why I started. I wanted to build a future that offered them stability, security, and the confidence to pursue their own dreams.

Today, I am proud to say I serve as an educational consultant and assistive technology specialist. In this role, I work collaboratively with a team to develop systems and strategies that ensure students receive the necessary accommodations to succeed. I'm also stepping into a new role as a psychology professor at a local college here in Georgia. This opportunity allows me to teach, inspire, and empower the next generation.

To anyone aspiring to become a doctor, I offer this: keep going. Know your why and hold on to it tightly. Pursue your goals with faith, determination, and a relentless desire to become the best version of yourself. There will be challenges, but there will also be victories. And when you reach that finish line, you'll look back and realize—you were becoming the person you were meant to be all along.

With love and encouragement,

Dr. La Toya S. Glenn

"

"Pursue your goals with faith, determination, and a relentless desire to become the best version of yourself."

"Be strong and courageous. Do not be afraid; do not be discouraged, for the Lord your God will be with you wherever you go."

Joshua 1:9

CHAPTER 3

DR. ANGELICA A. DAVIS

 An educator, mentor, and passionate advocate for student growth and community empowerment. Since beginning her journey in education in 2018, she has committed herself to helping children unlock their full potential, from guiding students through challenges in math and reading. Each moment in her career has been marked by patience, purpose, and the belief that every child has a voice worth hearing.

Beyond the classroom, Dr. Davis is deeply involved in serving her community. She volunteers and mentors with various organizations across the Charlotte area, dedicating her time and heart to supporting young people and families in need. A deep sense of responsibility drives her work and love for her community, and she carries this same spirit into every endeavor.

When she's not teaching or volunteering, Angelica enjoys reading, hiking, and embracing life's spontaneous adventures. A true traveler at heart, she finds inspiration in exploring new places and cultures, always seeking new stories, new lessons, and new ways to grow.

Dr. Angelica Alicia Davis continues to lead with compassion, curiosity, and an unwavering commitment to making a meaningful difference — one student, one moment, and one journey at a time.

Roots and Resilience: A Childhood Wrapped in Love

Growing up in St. Petersburg, Florida, was a beautiful experience. Though I was considered poor, perhaps with a hint of middle class, I never felt deprived. My grandmother, who raised me, made sure I always had what I needed. She worked as a housekeeper for a wealthy family, and no matter how hard she worked, she always made time to pour love, wisdom, and the value of education into me.

My childhood was carefree, filled with laughter and unforgettable memories. I was a bit of a tomboy and spent most of my days outside, exploring the world around me. Back then, a single dollar could go a long way, and life felt simple, joyful, and full of possibility.

As I sit and reflect, I realize just how grateful I am. I didn't have everything, but I had enough—and most importantly, I had love. My childhood was truly a gift.

From Setback to Purpose: The Moment I Chose the Doctoral Path

I knew I wanted to pursue my doctoral degree when I recognized how deeply the education system was failing our children, especially African American students. That realization wasn't just academic; it was personal. I, too, was failed by the system in third grade. I had to repeat the year, and no one truly advocated for me. That moment stayed with me.

Years later, as a teacher, I saw those same patterns in my classroom— bright students being overlooked, misunderstood, and underserved. I knew they needed a voice, not just inside the classroom, but beyond it.

They needed someone to fight for them, just as I once wished someone had fought for me. While working on my master's degree, I took a course on education law and policy. That class opened my eyes to the historic injustices African American students have endured—and how, despite everything, we still rise. It was then that I committed to join the

5% of African American women who hold a doctoral degree and to become a leader who advocates for equity and change.

More Than a Title: Why I Chose the Highest Step

Pursuing a terminal degree wasn't about chasing a title—it was about fulfilling a purpose. I thought about the little girl I used to be, the one who struggled, who was labeled, and who almost got lost in the cracks. I wanted to become the person she needed. I also thought about my students—the ones I taught in classrooms where resources were low but potential was high. I saw their brilliance, their dreams, and their determination. I wanted to be a mirror for them, a living example of what's possible.

Earning my doctorate meant I could do more than just teach—it meant I could lead, advocate, and create change from within the system. I wanted to be a force for transformation, not just for myself, but for every student who dared to dream beyond their circumstances.

A Purpose Found in Detours: How I Discovered My True Calling

Life didn't take me where I thought it would, but it brought me exactly where I needed to be. I originally set out to pursue a career in healthcare, earning an Associate's degree and working as a home health aide. While the work was meaningful, I knew in my heart it wasn't my true calling. I later transitioned into Human Resources, earned a Bachelor's in Business Management, and began a Master's program focused on Higher Education.

Then, I stepped into the classroom, and everything changed.

Teaching became my passion. I found joy and purpose in supporting students, particularly those in underserved communities. I saw the real-life challenges they carried—and I recognized their brilliance despite it all. That experience awakened something deeper in me. I wanted to do more. I needed to do more. And that desire led me to pursue my doctoral degree in education.

Every job, every step, and every degree brought me closer to discovering my purpose. And now, I walk confidently in it.

From Breakdown to Breakthrough: My Doctoral Journey

Whew—what a journey.

The beginning of my doctoral program was relatively smooth, but as I progressed, the real challenges began. I had to change my research topic multiple times. I wanted a committee that reflected my identity, so I selected a Hispanic woman and an African American man, hoping for balance and understanding.

Unfortunately, it didn't go as planned, and I felt defeated.

Imagine completing Chapter One of your dissertation, only to be told to start over with a completely different topic. I was embarrassed, discouraged, and emotionally exhausted. But after a heart-to-heart with my committee, I understood their concerns. I took two weeks to regroup and came back with a new topic: "Advancing to Leadership: African American Women in Higher Education."

That topic changed everything.

Even then, I faced challenges. I had to adjust my language, soften my tone, and learn how to tell hard truths in ways that welcomed readers in, rather than pushing them away. It took six months to get my proposal accepted. But once it was, I moved forward with confidence. I conducted my research, completed my writing, and defended my dissertation in November 2023, finishing the entire process in just 11 months. I leaned on my friends and my faith. I grew spiritually, and I clung to scriptures like Proverbs 27:17: "Iron sharpens iron," and trusted that God was using every hardship to refine me. Earning my doctorate wasn't just an academic milestone—it was a personal transformation. And every moment was worth it.

Fuel for the Climb: Who and What Motivated Me

When I think about what truly motivated me, it wasn't a single person—it was a version of myself. My younger self. The little girl who once struggled to pass the third grade, who felt left behind before she had even started. I carried her with me every step of the way. I worked for her, fought for her, believed in her. She reminded me that failure is not the end—it's the beginning of a comeback.

I was also blessed with an incredible circle of friends who carried me through the hardest moments. When I couldn't see the light, they reminded me of my strength. They helped edit chapters, planned nights out when I needed a break, and constantly poured love into me.

And then there was my grandmother—my north star. Her wisdom, her sacrifice, and her belief in the power of education became the foundation I stood on. Her words, "Aim high," still guide me.

That combination—my younger self, my friends, and the legacy of my grandmother—became the fuel that drove me to keep climbing.

Celebrating Every Step: My Doctoral Wins

During my doctoral journey, the victories came in many forms. I passed classes, gained committee approval, and received feedback that moved me forward. These small wins were major to me. In a process that often felt slow and uncertain, they were powerful reminders that I was still progressing.

But my biggest wins?

Walking across that stage. Being called "Doctor." I am seeing my research published and made available to others. Knowing that my voice, my story, and my scholarship would outlive me—that was everything. These weren't just academic wins. They were deeply personal. They represented resilience, healing, and the realization of a dream far bigger than myself.

Faith Forward: What Got Me to the Finish Line

Without question, it was God who carried me across the finish line.

In my darkest moments—when the feedback was hard, the deadlines overwhelming, and my spirit heavy—He was there. He never left me. He wrapped me in peace when I felt broken and gave me strength when I had none left to give.

And my village—my incredible friends—were the hands and hearts of that divine support. They loved me through my struggles, reminded me of my worth, and refused to let me give up.

It wasn't just willpower that got me to the end. It was grace. It was faith. It was love in action.

A New Chapter: Where I Am Now

In the final year of my doctoral journey, I made a difficult decision—I left the K–12 classroom after five years of fulfilling experience. Teaching had become my calling, but to complete what I started, I needed to shift my focus.

Today, I serve as the Department Administrator for the Engineering Department in Higher Education. It's a new space, a different kind of classroom—but it's still rooted in purpose. I continue to grow, lead, and mentor, especially for students and professionals who look like me. Although I'm no longer teaching in the traditional sense, I remain an educator. I still show up, still pour into others, and still carry the same mission: to inspire, uplift, and lead.

This chapter is about expansion. It's about stepping into new rooms and making space for others to follow. I'm not done yet—I'm just getting started.

For the Dreamers: A Letter to Aspiring Doctors

To every aspiring doctor—whether you're just beginning or deep in the journey—I want you to hear this: Keep going.

It will be hard. There will be nights when the words won't come, and days when you question if it's all worth it. But it is. Every step, every sacrifice, every tear is shaping you into who you're meant to be.

Invite God into the process. He'll be your anchor when everything else feels unstable. Let your faith lead you. He sees the end, even when you can't.

Build your tribe. Surround yourself with people who remind you of your strength, who speak life into your dreams, and who help you carry the load when it gets too heavy.

And above all—remember your "why." Hold onto it. Let it fuel you.

The title "Doctor" is more than a credential. It's a testimony. It says, "I didn't quit. I believed. I endured."

So walk boldly. The world needs your brilliance, your courage, your truth.

With love and belief in you always,

A Fellow Dreamer Who Made It

"

"It wasn't just willpower that got me to the end. It was grace. It was faith. It was love in action."

"But they that wait upon the Lord shall renew their strength; they shall mount up with wings as eagles; they shall run, and not be weary; they shall walk, and not faint."

Isaiah 40:31

CHAPTER 4

ALICIA SMALLS, MPH, MA, CCC-SLP, CBIST, CDP, LSVT-C

Fear Was the Beginning; Purpose Was the Promise: My Journey to the Doctorate. I didn't always see myself as a "doctor." For a long time, I saw fear, fear of not being enough, of being the only one in the room, of failing under the weight of my own expectations. Yet even in the quietest moments of doubt, I carried a truth that became my compass: "You belong in whatever room you set your feet in." That belief didn't erase the fear, but it gave me the faith to move anyway. And with each step, from imposter syndrome to acceptance, from burnout to breakthrough, I learned that fear might start the story, but it doesn't get to write my ending. Faith builds the bridge, but purpose? Purpose keeps you walking. This is my story of becoming, of belonging, and of boldly claiming space in a world I once thought was too big for me.

Foundations: My Childhood Story

I was raised primarily by my mother, though my father remained present in my life. Both of my parents emphasized the importance of education from an early age. My mother worked three jobs to care for my brother and me, and she would always say, "The only thing I require from you is that you try." In our home, perseverance wasn't just encouraged, it was required. Whether through the quiet strength of a hardworking parent, the resilience of a community that made something out of nothing, or the unspoken understanding that education was the path forward, my childhood was rooted in survival, faith, and quiet ambition. I didn't have a silver spoon, but I had a foundation built on grit. As a child, I dreamed of becoming a lawyer. I was glued to shows like Matlock, JAG, Night Court, and Ally McBeal. I admired the way attorneys built their cases, uncovered the truth, and confidently presented their arguments in court. The suit and briefcase were just the icing on the cake. That dream stayed with me well into high school. Throughout high school, I worked closely with my guidance counselor to explore my future. With a strong GPA, membership in the National Honor Society, and numerous academic honors, I shared with her my interest in law. Recognizing my drive, she nominated me for the National Youth Leadership Forum on Law in Washington, D.C., an incredible opportunity to meet representatives from top law schools and connect with national policymakers. I was excited, and I seriously considered the legal path.

However, as I began researching the profession more deeply, I became concerned about the potential risks and demands of the field. Slowly, my passion started to shift. When I told my parents I had decided against pursuing law, they were understandably disappointed. Still, they supported my decision so long as I followed a path I loved and remained committed to academic excellence. After graduating from high school, I enrolled in an Associate of Science degree program at a technical college in my state. The program offered a bridge to a four-year university, allowing me to complete core courses at a lower cost while I explored my career options. I knew I wanted to earn a bachelor's degree, but I wasn't certain of my major yet.

By the time I completed my associate's degree, I had narrowed my focus to two fields: medical school or a related field in rehabilitation. I ultimately applied to the Bachelor of Science in Exercise Science program at the University of South Carolina. I was drawn to its variety of foundational tracks: Scientific Foundations, Health Promotion Education and Behavior (HPEB), Public Health, and Health Fitness. I chose the

Scientific Foundations track because it included the core prerequisites for both medical school and most rehabilitation programs, allowing me to keep both paths open as I continued to discern my purpose. Just as I began settling into this new direction, life shifted in ways I could never have anticipated.

The Path Before the Program

During my bachelor's degree program, life took an unexpected and heartbreaking turn. I

experienced the tragic loss of my brother, who was my best friend, and the very next day, I went into premature labor and gave birth to my son three months early. The weight of grief and the shock of early motherhood collided all at once. I took a semester off to begin healing, regroup, and adjust to this entirely new chapter. That season of my life forced me to reevaluate everything. Loss has a way of doing that. It stripped away the illusion of certainty and pushed me to reconsider my purpose, my direction, and what really mattered.

In that same chapter of life, I endured two of the most devastating losses of my life. I lost my grandmother, my heart, my prayer warrior, and one of my fiercest supporters. The following year, I lost my father. His love for me was quiet but steadfast, and his pride in my achievements was always evident. Someone once said that grief is love with no place to go, and in that season, my heart felt full and hollow at the same time. Their absence left an ache I couldn't ignore, but it also became a source of quiet strength. I carried them with me into every decision I made, every step forward.

At the time, instead of applying to medical school or a rehabilitation program as originally planned, I chose to pursue a master's in public health. I believed it was a way to contribute meaningfully to health and wellness on a broader scale. But soon after completing the degree, I realized something was missing. I just didn't want to analyze the data; I needed a human connection. I longed for the face-to-face moments that brought impact to life. I began exploring new paths and toured the University of St. Augustine's Doctor of Physical Therapy program. It was an important visit, but as I weighed the structure and expectation of the program, I realized it wasn't the right fit. I was back to the drawing board.

Then one day, during a routine speech therapy session for my son, I found myself watching his Speech-Language Pathologist closely. She was one of the first Black SLPs I had ever met. One afternoon, she turned to me and asked, "Have you ever thought about becoming a speech-language pathologist?" I didn't. I told her I hadn't even heard of the profession before my son started receiving services. She smiled and said, "I think you'd make a great one." Her words stayed with me. A year later, I applied to a Speech-Language Pathology graduate program. I wanted a fresh start, so I chose not to return to my undergraduate university. Instead, I applied to South Carolina State University, my very first HBCU experience. And oh, what an experience it was. The lessons I learned and the connections I made there reshaped me.

One of the most impactful influences during my time there was Dr. Tanya Wilson. As both a professor and mentor, Dr. Wilson guided me with rigor, compassion, and purpose. She constantly pushed me to think critically, advocate fiercely, and embrace my voice. It was Dr. Wilson who encouraged me to do my first public speaking engagement through the Speech Uncensored podcast, reassuring me that my voice and my experience mattered. That moment sparked a chain reaction of opportunities that I never imagined, from national panels to podcast hosting and beyond. Her love and unwavering support were absolutely amazing; there was never a moment when I didn't feel encouraged to grow and stretch beyond my comfort zone. Dr. Wilson made me feel truly seen.

I was also incredibly fortunate to receive support from Dr. Nia Johnson, whose mentorship extended beyond the classroom. She frequently invited me to guest lectures and to speak to organizations she was affiliated with, allowing me to grow professionally and expand my network. Dr. Johnson consistently created space for me to be seen, heard, and valued; something I will always carry with me. Her consistent belief in my abilities reinforced that I belonged in academic and leadership spaces. These two phenomenal women not only mentored me academically, but they also modeled what leadership, integrity, and community impact truly look like. Their support solidified my decision to pursue a path beyond clinical work and to step into a space where I could shake the table, advocate, educate, and lead.

After completing my Master's in Speech-Language Pathology, I began working clinically with individuals with traumatic brain injury, stroke, and progressive neurodegenerative diseases. I served as the lead SLP at a regional rehabilitation hospital, where I began mentoring students, delivering guest lectures, and collaborating on patient-centered initiatives. I quickly realized that I didn't just want to provide care, I wanted to improve it. This clarity led me to pursue a PhD in Exercise Science with a concentration in

Rehabilitation Science and Neuroscience. I wanted to be at the forefront of research; to investigate the gaps I saw daily in clinical practice, and to develop solutions for the communities I serve. Every challenge I faced, every personal loss, pivot, and redirection had built the foundation I would stand on as a future doctor.

Why I Chose a Terminal Degree

The doctorate was never just a degree. It was a declaration. A promise to myself that I would push the boundaries of what was possible for my patients, my community, and the generations coming behind me. As a practicing speech-language pathologist, I often worked with individuals recovering from traumatic brain injury (TBI), many of whom were also affected by seizures and strokes, which contributed to further cognitive decline. Watching my patients struggle with their new normal and watching their families grieve the person they once knew stayed with me. Those moments weren't just clinical; they were deeply human. Over time, I found myself constantly searching for the latest research, hoping to diagnose better and treat the complex deficits these patients faced. It became clear to me that traditional neuroimaging tools often failed to capture the subtle, yet devastating, cognitive-communicative challenges that many TBI survivors experience. There were too many gaps, too many things we didn't fully understand. The literature was growing, and I wanted to help accelerate that growth.

That desire to bridge gaps in care wasn't new. During my master's program in Speech-Language Pathology, I had a unique opportunity to conduct research alongside an audiologist in rural South Carolina. We studied noise-induced hearing loss in farmers who frequently used heavy farming equipment. What we found was striking: prolonged noise exposure was not only associated with auditory decline but also linked to elevated blood pressure levels in this population. Interestingly, when farmers used ear protection consistently, their blood pressure readings decreased. This work helped me recognize the intricate relationship between auditory health, systemic health, and environmental exposure. It also sparked my curiosity in how sensory processing, particularly hearing, intersects with broader cognitive and neurological function.

Between the patients I treated and the research questions that kept me up at night, I knew I needed more training to ask and answer these big questions. I just didn't want to treat symptoms. I aimed to develop improved tools, contribute to scientific advancements, and transform the approach to TBI diagnoses and care. I didn't want to just be part of the conversation; I wanted to reshape it. Pursuing a PhD in Exercise Science with a concentration in Rehabilitation Science and Neuroscience became my next right step. These experiences directly influenced the focus of my doctoral research. I became increasingly interested in how auditory changes, such as tinnitus and sensorineural hearing loss, interact with cognitive symptoms in individuals with a history of concussion or mild traumatic brain injury. I wanted to move beyond what could be seen on standard imaging. That's when I turned to functional neuroimaging. My current research leverages fNIRS to examine the dynamic interplay between hearing function, cognition, and concussion outcomes. I am especially focused on vulnerable and high-risk populations, specifically pediatric populations, and military personnel whose cumulative exposure to noise, head impacts, and high-performance demands may contribute to long-term neurological changes. This work enables me to integrate my clinical insights with innovative tools, advancing our understanding, diagnosis, and treatment of brain injury in real-world settings. And most of all, I wanted to show others that you can be both a healer and scholar, a dreamer and doer, a woman of faith and a woman of science.

This commitment to innovation and impact was the compass that guided me in the next chapter of my journey: the doctoral program itself. While my research gave me a renewed sense of purpose, the path to carrying it out was anything but easy. The work was meaningful, but the process of becoming a scholar, while also navigating life's many demands, would test every ounce of my faith, strength, and resilience.

Doctoral Life: The Trials and Triumphs

My first semester of doctoral training was one of the most demanding and disorienting periods of my academic journey. I was balancing multiple roles from working on campus, maintaining my position at the hospital, taking a full course load, serving as the clinical research coordinator, and collecting data weekly at the Pediatric Concussion Clinic for ongoing lab projects. And above all, I was still a single mom. The weight of it all felt nearly unbearable at times. The constant juggling act between deadlines, responsibilities, and motherhood placed me in a difficult headspace. There were moments when I questioned whether I had made the right decision, whether I could truly handle this. What they don't often tell you is that choosing a doctoral environment with strong, consistent support is not just helpful, it's critical.

Unfortunately, the support that was marketed to me during my admissions process did not match the reality I encountered once enrolled. I was the only minority in my lab, and that reality came with its own set of challenges. I experienced repeated microaggressions from a fourth-year doctoral student, a post-doctoral researcher, and a previous graduate of the lab. One instance remains etched in my memory:

I was told directly by another faculty member in my lab that I wouldn't be a strong enough candidate for a prestigious minority grant geared toward clinicians and scientists, that my Caucasian male mentor would be a better fit for it. It was both invalidating and infuriating.

Vital information was often withheld from me or delayed in delivery. On several occasions, I discovered grants or fellowships I was eligible for and presented them to my mentor, only to be met with reluctance or outright refusal to write letters of recommendation. Despite frequent compliments on my writing from other professors in the department, I was often told in my lab that I was "not good enough" or "not ready" for certain opportunities. Even when I requested hands-on neuroimaging training that was

originally promised as part of my doctoral development, I received no structured guidance. I had to take it upon myself to find mentorship and training through other faculty who were willing to support my growth.

The disconnect between what was originally promised and what I experienced left me bruised, feeling isolated, and overwhelmed in an already high-pressure environment. I had to learn quickly how to advocate for myself, seek out my own support systems, and set boundaries that protected both my goals and my well-being. Despite the trials, those early challenges forged in me a deeper resilience and focus. I realized that while the system around me may have fallen short, I could still rise. I was not here by accident; I was here on purpose with a purpose. I had earned this seat, and I would do whatever it took to remain in it and make it to the finish line.

Fuel for the Climb: What Kept Me Going

In the moments when I felt like I was running empty, when deadlines loomed, when there were critical hospital visits for my son, or the weight of my responsibilities left me questioning everything, I returned to my "why." My son was and continues to be my greatest motivation. Every paper I wrote, every meeting I attended, every research hour logged was with him in mind. I wanted him to see, firsthand, what perseverance looks like. I wanted him to know that he was never a limitation to my dreams, but the reason I pressed forward. The legacy I'm building is not just for me, it's for him. The memory of my brother also fueled me. Losing him altered my life forever, but his spirit shows up in the quiet moments, reminding me that life is fragile and purpose is urgent. That grief gave me clarity, and in many ways, it became a catalyst. My mentors, especially Dr. Tanya Wilson, Dr. Nia Johnson, and Dr. Vanessa Coleman-Lebby, were lifelines. They saw things in me before I saw them in myself. Their encouragement was more than academic; it was deeply personal. They reminded me that I belonged, even when the environment tried to convince me otherwise. But it wasn't just the mentors who carried me; it was my village. My friends became my breath when I felt like I was drowning. Jaleese and Sabrea showed up for me, not just in spirit but in presence; sitting with me in hospital rooms when my son underwent emergency surgery, lifting me with their love. My high school friend Shanay covered me in prayer and reminded me, "Sis, when you win, I win."

My dear friend Logan sat with me during the tears and whispered truth over my life, telling me, "Life is full of peaks and valleys, but you will make it to the top of the mountain." Victoria, my college best friend, never let me forget to love myself and to actually live while I chased these dreams. Charvette listened to every twist and turn of this doctoral journey and always reminded me to finish strong.

Teranesha brought laughter into my lowest days; her gift of joy always arrived right on time. And Morgan and Bethany, steadfast and faithful, constantly kept me in their prayers and reminded me how proud they were of me. And then, there was faith. Faith that my steps were ordered. Faith that I was built for this. Faith that even when the process was painful, the purpose was still intact. I leaned on prayer, on journaling, and on small moments of grace that appeared just when I needed them most. I also leaned into therapy when life became foggy, and I needed help putting things into perspective. That period required me to reevaluate my "why." No one really tells you how lonely the doctoral journey can be. It's isolating. Your experience is totally unique to you. And even though I was achieving things most PhD students don't — board positions on two prestigious organizations, a strong GPA, maintaining three jobs, publishing an abstract in the Brain Injury Journal, giving international conference presentations, and numerous other speaking engagements — something still felt missing.

I remember my therapist asking me in one session, "Are you proud of yourself and all that you've accomplished despite what you've been through and are still going through?" I answered honestly: "No." I wasn't proud of myself because I had to fight for every step. That afternoon, I sat with what had transpired in therapy and began to deeply reevaluate my purpose. One thing I've always done is save every card given to me by friends, family, and mentors. I keep them on my bookshelf as gentle reminders that I am loved. One card stood out that day, it was from one of my mentors. The cover read, "Don't Forget You've Got People." Tears welled in my eyes. I had forgotten. This journey can make you feel so isolated that you lose sight of your village. That night, I leaned extra heavy into my faith. I opened my Bible, searching for something to hold on to. Two scriptures stood out:

Micah 7:7-8- "But as for me, I watch in hope for the Lord, I wait for God my Savior; my God will hear me. Do not gloat over me, my enemy! Though I have fallen, I will rise. Though I sit in darkness, the Lord will be my light."

Isaiah 41:10- "So do not fear, for I am with you; do not be dismayed, for I am your God. I will strengthen you and help you; I will uphold you with my righteous right hand."

That same night, I played my gospel playlist, one of the few things that helped me reset.

On repeat was You Know My Name by Tasha Cobbs Leonard. There's a verse in that song that still sits in my soul: "No fire can burn me. No battle can turn me. No mountain can stop me. 'Cause You hold my hand. And now I'm walking in Your victory. 'Cause Your power is within me. No giant can defeat me. 'Cause You hold my hand." That verse reminded me of a truth I had nearly forgotten; I wasn't walking this journey alone. I was being held by something greater, guided by a force that had already seen me through every valley.

That song became an anthem, an anchor on the days I felt like I had nothing left to give. Support didn't always come in the traditional form, but I found it in friends who cheered me on, in colleagues who affirmed my work, and in patients whose stories reminded me why I do what I do. It was this patchwork of love, legacy, belief, therapy, and faith that kept me grounded and moving.

Celebrating the Wins

Eventually, I realized that even in my hardest seasons, I was still moving forward and that movement mattered. For a long time, I was so focused on surviving that I never paused to honor how far I'd come. But as I reflected on the journey, I began to see the quiet milestones I'd achieved: maintaining a strong GPA while raising my son, balancing three jobs, and earning leadership roles on prestigious boards where I turned lived experiences into advocacy. I had my first abstract accepted to the Brain Injury Journal, presented at an international conference, and spoke on stages I once only dreamed about. These weren't just resume lines; they were reminders that I was making an impact, even when I didn't always feel seen.

Recognizing my own growth allowed me to become a mirror for others. I mentored younger students, giving them the kind of guidance I once needed. Dr. Wilson deeply inspired that part of my journey. Her mentorship changed the trajectory of my life, and I knew I needed to pay it forward. One of my proudest wins has been mentoring my student, Marie. From the moment we connected, I saw pieces of myself in her: the ambition, the quiet strength, and the unspoken weight of navigating hard things with grace. Like me, she faced challenges that could have easily derailed her dreams, but she did not stop. She will be graduating this June with her master's degree, and watching her grow has been one of the most affirming experiences of my doctoral journey. Celebrating the wins did not come naturally. I was so used to pushing through, to surviving, that pausing felt foreign, almost indulgent. But now, I recognize their importance. Each achievement is a stone in the foundation I'm building, not just for myself, but for every person who sees a piece of their story in mine. Each milestone is proof that rising from hardship is possible, that excellence can grow from broken ground, and that purpose can be forged in pain. My journey is not just about the letters behind my name; it is about creating a path wide enough for others to walk through with less fear, more hope, and a deep belief in their worth.

With each step, each hard-earned milestone, I have come to understand that this journey was never just about arriving; it was about becoming. And now, as I approach the final stretch,

That growth feels undeniable.

Approaching the Finish Line

Now, I find myself standing in the final stretch of this journey. I have not yet defended my dissertation; I am preparing to submit it for a proposal. And while I am still deep at work, I can finally see the horizon. There is a new stillness in me, not from the absence of challenges, but from having endured enough of them to know I can rise again. This closing chapter has been marked by clarity, intentionality, and self-trust. I have sharpened my research focus, discovered my voice as a scholar, and most importantly, learned how to protect my time, my peace, and my purpose.

There is a kind of resolve that comes from surviving the middle, the messy, uncertain middle, where growth happens in the dark and break-throughs are often quiet. I no longer feel the need to prove that I belong here; I know that I do. That knowing has become my foundation. Of course, the challenges have not disappeared. The deadlines still come fast, revisions can be relentless, and meetings pile onto already packed weeks. But I meet these pressures differently now. I have developed a rhythm, one that prioritizes both excellence and sustainability. I have learned that rest is part of the work, and boundaries are a form of self-re-spect. I have stopped chasing perfection and started honoring progress.

What keeps me going is the vision. A vision not just of earning a title or hanging a degree on the wall, but using everything I have learned to make a real, tangible impact. I see myself standing before students who look like me, advocating for brain injury survivors whose voices are often left out of the research conversation, and leading with a blend of compassion, data, and lived experience. This journey has become bigger than me; it's a call to serve, to mentor, to build pathways where none existed before.

The work I am doing is no longer just about reaching the end. It is about setting a precedent and building a legacy. I may not be at the finish line yet, but every step forward affirms this truth: I'm closer than I have ever been, and I am becoming exactly who I was always meant to be.

Where I Am Now

Everything I have endured, learned, and become has led me to this moment, a space where my lived experience, clinical work, and scientific inquiry now align with purpose. Today, I am a doctoral candidate preparing to propose my dissertation in the final year of my PhD program in Exercise Science with a focus on Rehabilitation Science and Neuroscience. I am a clinician-scientist, educator, advocate, and speaker. I collaborate clinically with individuals affected by traumatic brain injury, stroke, and neurodegenerative conditions, while also serving as a Clinical Research Coordinator and Graduate Research Assistant.

My research now focuses on improving how we assess and support individuals with brain injuries, especially those in vulnerable groups like military personnel and the pediatric population. Using tools like fNIRS and EEG-ERP, I aim to deepen our understanding of how hearing loss, tinnitus, and cognitive changes interact after concussion. This work is about more than data; it is about advancing clinical care and ensuring that underserved communities are not left behind in the research conversation.

Beyond the research, I am deeply committed to mentoring aspiring clinicians and scientists, especially those from backgrounds historically excluded from academic spaces. I serve on national and international professional boards, advocate for health equity, and speak nationally on brain injury, culturally responsive care, and creating spaces of inclusion in healthcare and academia. Each role I hold is a reflection of the purpose that fuels me. I want others to see that it is possible to lead with both compassion and rigor, to ground science in the community, and to turn pain into purpose.

Where I am now is not a final destination; it is a platform. A platform to build upon, give back, and continue growing. I carry this work forward not just as a professional calling, but as a personal mission: to open doors, build bridges, and leave every space better than I found it.

A Letter to Aspiring Doctors

Dear Future Doctor,

I want you to hold onto something I wish someone had told me more often: your journey is valid, your pace is enough, your voice is powerful, and your God is might! This path will test you. It will stretch you mentally, emotionally, and spiritually, but it will also reveal your resilience in ways you never imagined. There will be days when the finish line feels out of reach, when imposter syndrome whispers lies, and when you wonder if you really belong here.

Keep going anyway.

When the weight of it all feels too much and your "why" begins to fade, know this: stillness is not failure. Sometimes, the most powerful thing you can do is pause, breathe, and realign. Give yourself permission to reset. And when you're ready, take one more step, just one. That's all it takes. If you ever forget who you are, lean into your faith. Lean into your community. Lean into the calling that led you here in the first place. Let the people who love you remind you of your light. Celebrate every win, especially the quiet ones. Rest without guilt. Speak up. Ask for help.

Protect your peace. And always, always remember this:

You belong in every room you step into.

You are not behind. You are not an impostor. You are not invisible. You are becoming.

Fear doesn't mean stop.

Faith means keep going.

And purpose? Purpose makes every step worth it.

With deep belief in you,

Alicia

"

"Sis, when you win, I win."

"For I know the plans I have for you," declares the Lord, "plans to prosper you and not to harm you, plans to give you hope and a future."

Jeremiah 29:11

CHAPTER 5

DR. NA'KHIA S. WASHINGTON

 "Let me be the first to say, Congratulations, Dr. Washington, Welcome to the Academy." When I heard those words from my Dissertation Chair, I lifted my hands, bowed my head, giving thanks and glory to God, as tears freely flowed down my face. For the first time in my life, I didn't attempt to wipe the tears away, nor did I attempt to hide the fact that I was shedding tears in front of a 'Zoom room' of 50-plus people, the biggest audience that my committee said they'd ever seen. Not only were the tears I released tears of joy, but those tears also represented just about every emotion that I experienced through my doctoral journey. Emotions such as fear, anger, inadequacy, frustration, grief, anxiety, contempt, overwhelm, aggravation, and apprehension, to name a few. Ironically, as I allowed those tears to fall, not only did the heaviness lift, but the tension headache that I had for what seemed like two straight years had instantly subsided.

As I struggled to get myself together, my Subject Matter Expert asked me if I had anything to say before we engaged in post-defense dialogue. The only thing I could muster up in that moment was "Thank You Jesus"...in that very brief moment, 'my soul looked back and wondered how I got over', because my journey hasn't been an easy one. No, I didn't live a life of poverty, and we didn't struggle to make ends meet, but when you have a God-ordained assignment on your life, the struggle, as they say, is real.

Growing up as the youngest of three from a strong ministry family, who had not only committed their lives to God but also to service and education, I knew that I'd pursue a terminal degree of some sort. While I was pushed, encouraged, and supported in my home and by my family, I can't say that was my testimony outside of my home and extended family. A product of the public school system, I can say my experience has been pretty good. However, it wasn't until I attended a predominantly white high school and was told by one of the school's guidance counselors what they were called at the time- that "I didn't have what it would take to go to college for law". Although this wasn't my assigned counselor, the fact that she was someone who was placed in authority to help develop, nurture and guide young people to make decisions for their future tell me, one who had been on the honor roll my entire school career, tell me that I didn't have what it took to go to college definitely bothered me.

I shared the experience with a friend of mine who didn't look like me, nor was she as strong a student as I was, and I'd learned that she, too, had an exchange with that same counselor; however, she was given tips, strategies, scholarship information, and extra support. Mind you, she wasn't her counselor either. We were both assigned the same counselor as freshmen because of our last names. He was an amazing counselor, but unfortunately, he was out with the flu at the time. His caseload was split between the two other counselors until he returned. However, the damage had been done, and my confidence had taken a major blow.

I didn't share this encounter with my assigned counselor upon his return, but I did share it with my family about two to three weeks later, and it was that moment that changed the trajectory of my life forever. It was this moment that my family sat me down for 'the talk'. This is the conversation that every African American family in America must make an effort to ensure survival and success in various situations and settings. This encounter was when I was forced to realize that no matter how hard I work, no matter the grades I get, it will never be good enough for a society built on the backs of my ancestors, but rooted in racism. So in that moment, I learned that I had to be twice as good and work ten times harder just to prove that I not only worked hard for where I am, but I deserve the perks that come with hard work and dedication, and that I should not apologize, nor should I shrink because of it. While I continued to be a hard worker, that not shrinking part didn't come until later...much later...like recently. More about that as you continue to read.

I went on to earn an Associate's Degree from the local community college, after having to take time off due to an emergency kidney operation, and a Bachelor's Degree from one of the top universities in the tri-state area. By now, I was teaching, but I wasn't sure if I wanted to go into school administration, school counseling, or private practice. Then I began to take note of some things. I noticed how the school counselor, who didn't look like the students she served, was treating the students who attended our school, and it took me right back to my high school days. I made a vow that day that I would never allow a student to feel the way I felt by a member of the school community who was meant to help guide, nurture, and support them. It was that memory that drove my decision to return to grad school for school counseling.

While in grad school, I immediately knew that I was going to pursue a terminal degree; it was just the question of 'in what discipline?' As I began to get some small opportunities to present here and there in the education realm and in church settings as well as being tapped for consultation for various educational issues and hot topics, I decided a degree in Educational Leadership was the best way for me to go.

I also realized the need for a terminal degree for me because as an educator, especially an African American educator who had the honor of being named and recognized as Pennsylvania's School Counselor of the Year, and additionally had been invited back to serve as an adjunct professor at my beloved alma mater, there were times when I had been the most qualified person in the room but had been overlooked or ignored for, I'll say two reasons, one-because I was an African American woman and two-because I didn't have the terminal degree. So I applied and was accepted into my doctoral program, and the rest, as they say, was history. But let me tell you, my time in my program was not easy. The coursework leading up to actual dissertation writing was a breeze, but 'life was lifing' for me.

In January of 2019, during my second year of my program, I was injured in a freak accident where a heater exploded in my home, and I sustained second and third-degree burns over half of my body, where I had been out of commission for a while but was still able to complete my coursework. Then, in 2020, we were all impacted by the pandemic. Honestly, the pandemic was a very productive time for me as I had so many other life commitments during that time, such as ministry, coaching, and my small business. However, this was the time I was actually able to lock in and get the coursework done ahead of my projected timeline and proceed with the writing of my dissertation.

My advisor set up an introductory meeting for me with my chair. Before settling on a topic, my then chair, a caucasian male, was very warm and open and sent various resources; however, once I decided that I wanted to research the impact that out-of-school suspensions have on African American females using critical race theory as my theoretical framework, he ghosted me. He became very hard to work with, and even suggested that I study something else. I struggled a bit with whether or not I should, in fact, change it, because after all, he was the 'expert', the one who was to serve as my mentor throughout this process, right? Because I was still very apprehensive about whether the topic should be changed, I did what I was taught to do...pray about it. After praying about it, I made the decision that I would in fact keep the topic, and reached out to my advisor to schedule a meeting to request a new chair, and as I was emailing her, I received an email from my then chair stating that he could no longer serve as my chair because "he was leaving the university." I later found out that that was a lie, but I couldn't have been more relieved because I honestly didn't feel that I would've gotten the support I needed. Then I met my new chair, a caucasian woman who was a retired school counselor. While the process with my new chair wasn't always smooth, I knew I needed to stand up for myself in certain situations because I felt like I was being academically hazed. Once we cleared the air, we were able to move forward and complete the process with a successful published dissertation and defense.

While I had a pretty good experience overall, I definitely have to say my mom, Mrs. Sandra Washington, and family (the Colbert and Ashe families) motivated me not only to pursue my terminal degree but to finish this journey. They've always set the bar high and maintained the standard of excellence for as long as I can remember. However, I didn't just have my family, I had a village of people; my Godmother, Dr. Terri-Lynne Alston who not only encouraged me along the way, but she also held my feet to the fire to ensure that I was making progress; my mentor, Dr. Karen Dickinson, who offered academic support and emotional support, making sure my SUDS levels were in tack and that I was taking care of na'Khia; my boss, Dr. William Hayes, who provided insight, he pushed me (boy did he push me), he challenged me, he was a thought partner and encouraged me to always maximize my potential; my friend, Josish "JoJo" Martin, who was such an encourager and listened when I needed an ear, but most importantly, his song "Run On" (download it on all streaming platforms) was on repeat, during those tearful nights of frustration, discouragement, inadequacy, and even anger at times. I must also say, I was made aware of The Woman Doctor Instagram at a very crucial time, and she was so very encouraging and helped me get across the finish line more than she realizes. However, none of what I did and would have even been possible if it had not been for my faith and my Savior.

So here I am now, a year later, serving as the Director of School Counseling at Boys' Latin of Philadelphia Charter School, a Counselor Educator at West Chester of Pennsylvania, a National Board Certified Counselor, an award-winning educator, a frequent conference presenter, a college and career coach, and a consultant.

As a new doctor, I would like to encourage aspiring doctors with these nuggets: if you have a dream, GO FOR IT!!! Don't allow the thoughts and opinions of others to deter or discourage you. Be prepared to sacrifice. You may have to change your lifestyle, miss out on some social things, and you certainly will endure many sleepless nights, but it will be worth it all once you hear "Congratulations, Doctor, Welcome to the Academy". People will not understand the sacrifices you will have to make, and they may even make slick comments, but that's when you must surround yourself with people who are already where you are trying to go. Remember, Imposter Syndrome is REAL, but 'you got this' and you deserve to be where you are...you've worked so hard to get here, so give yourself grace during those moments of uncertainty. Don't apologize for where you are. Don't shrink, don't cower down, and don't dim your light to be digestible to others...they can choke, respectfully!!! You've worked too hard not to share and enlighten your community with all that you've studied and researched!!! Finally, make sure that you take time for self-care and remember to ENJOY THE JOURNEY!!!

Many days, I wanted to quit, but I realized that God had and still has a plan and a purpose for my life, so quitting was never an option. God never starts to stop; He starts to finish. Being confident of this very thing, that he which hath begun a good work in you will perform it until the day of Jesus Christ. (Philippians 1:6)

Forever I remain,

Dr. na'Khia S. Washington, NCC

"

"You've worked so hard to get here, so give yourself grace during those moments of uncertainty."

"And we know that for those who love God all things work together for good, for those who are called according to his purpose."

Romans 8:28

CHAPTER 6

DR. ANNA I. FONDREN

 I grew up an only child in the Chicagoland area, raised by two parents who believed deeply in the power of education. My dad (now retired) was a locomotive engineer from St. Louis—one of nine kids and the only one to go to college. He arrived sight unseen by Greyhound, figuring it all out as he went. My mom, also a first-generation college student, grew up in Harvey, Illinois, a suburb on the outskirts of the south side of Chicago. She started at Illinois State, but after her mother passed, she transferred to Chicago State and earned her degree. My parents met, fell in love, got married, and had me.

Education was everything in our home. My mom would always say, "People can take everything from you, but never your education," and "Your child should go further than you." That mindset shaped everything. As a kid, I struggled with speech—those pesky "r" and "w" sounds. I spent years in speech therapy, embarrassed to be pulled from class every week. I also had a tough time with math. My parents were relentless in their support: tutoring at a teacher's home, Sylvan Learning Center, whatever it took. I'll never forget the 7th-grade teacher who looked me in the eye and said, "My kids are smarter than you." I came home crushed, feeling small, but my parents weren't about to let that slide. They showed up at the school, advocated for me fiercely, and by the next year, that teacher was gone. Ironically, he ended up teaching in a nearby school district where my cousin had him—and guess what? The complaints followed him there, too. That experience stuck with me, not because of what he said, but because it taught me early on that people will doubt you, project their own limitations onto you. But when you have the right people in your corner and a fire in your spirit, their words don't define your path—you do.

Looking back, I don't hold on to that moment with bitterness—I hold on to it as fuel. A reminder of how far I've come. Some days, I imagine running into him just to say, "Remember me? The girl you underestimated? You were wrong." Because today, I carry not just one degree, but multiple, and the title Doctor in front of my name. In high school, I thrived in honors classes (except math), joined clubs, played sports, and started believing in myself. I realized I didn't want to be in the medical field after one brutal honors chemistry class, but I still had big dreams. During my junior year, we toured colleges across Illinois. I wanted to go out of state, but my mom said, "You won't be able to come home whenever you want," and that settled it for me. I chose Illinois State University and majored in Criminal Justice, with law school in mind.

I never planned to pursue a PhD. In grad school, I had my heart set on law school—until I opened an LSAT prep book, didn't understand the instructions to the first question, and quietly closed that chapter. Around the same time, one of my professors said, "I see you excelling in a PhD program." I laughed it off, terrified of taking another statistics course and unsure of the path.

Graduation was approaching, and I had no job offers—just a few assistantships and part-time jobs on my résumé. After two breakups and a deep need for change, I decided to move out of Illinois. I had always dreamed of living in Houston and attending an HBCU, so I began my search. That's when I stumbled on Prairie View A&M University's PhD program in Juvenile Justice. It was February 23, 2019. The deadline to apply was March 1. I stayed up all night pulling my application together—essays, letters, transcripts—everything had to be mailed, no online submissions. I drove across town to the post office just before it closed.

Only my parents knew I applied, because PV was the only school I applied to. I didn't think I'd get in. Fast forward to May 2019: I was in a Houston hotel lobby with my parents when the email came in. The subject read "Admission Decision." I braced for a rejection, but instead saw: "Congratulations!" My parents' faces lit up with pure joy. My mom immediately picked up the phone, calling family and friends, proudly declaring to anyone who would listen, "My daughter is going to be a doctor!" Her voice was beaming with pride—it was a moment I'll never forget. I started that fall. The work was intense, and impostor syndrome hit hard. Then came the blow I never saw coming: In October, my mom was diagnosed with stage 4 cancer. The next day, my grandmother—my dad's mom, and the last living grandparent—passed away. I tried to keep up with school by calling my dad for updates during class breaks and flying back and forth. My professors told me to take a break. I couldn't. I knew if I stopped, I wouldn't return.

Before my mom passed on November 4, 2019, she looked at me and said, "Whatever happens, finish that degree," and "Please go to therapy." I promised I would. I took incompletes that semester, then doubled my course load to stay on track. When COVID hit, I temporarily moved back home, grieving and depressed. Most days, I couldn't get out of bed. I drank too much. I smiled around friends, but I was drowning. Back in Houston, the pain got worse. I even filled out the withdrawal forms… but never hit submit.

Eventually, I wrapped up my coursework and sat for comprehensive exams with my cohort just before spring 2022 kicked off—imposter syndrome, as always, close behind. While I was studying, I got the heartbreaking call that my great aunt, who was like a grandmother to me, had passed away. Not being able to attend her funeral shattered me. That spring, I was teaching an Intro to Criminal Justice course, and I truly loved it. I poured my heart into designing lessons, sharing real-life stories from Chicago, and challenging my students to avoid the pitfalls I once fell into. Then, right before class one day, I got the email: I passed all sections of my comprehensive exams. I laughed just to keep from crying in front of my students. It was a huge victory, but I knew what came next: the real battle—the dissertation writing became a battle—not because I lacked the skill (writing has always been one of my strengths), but because mentally, I just couldn't sit still long enough to focus. Anxiety, grief, self-doubt—they all showed up. Some days I couldn't write at all. Other days, opening my laptop felt like taking a sleeping pill. Still, I pushed through and made it to my prospectus defense. Just minutes before presenting, I learned my dad was in the ER, dangerously close to having a stroke.

I passed the defense, my dad ended up being fine, but my nerves were completely shot. Despite my professors' earlier advice to take a break—which I'd ignored—I eventually had to step back. What was meant to be a short pause turned into two years of silence. I stopped checking emails, deleted apps, and muted notifications. Watching others from my cohort graduate crushed me. All I could hear was my mom's voice reminding me: "Whatever happens, finish that degree."

More loss came—two aunts, a best friend. Life kept piling on. I finally kept my second promise to my mom and started therapy. It saved me. Slowly, I reconnected with my professors and got back on track. The fire was lit again. It was time. I had to finish. I had to graduate. With my dissertation chair confirming I'd graduate in May 2025, I locked in—tunnel vision. I poured everything into finishing, and on April 4th, I passed my final defense. I was nervous, but this time, I had tools from therapy to calm the storm.

Then came May 16th, 2025. At 29 years old, I walked across the stage as Dr. Anna Fondren. From doubting I'd get into the program to battling grief, anxiety, depression, and impostor syndrome—I made it.

This degree wasn't just academic. It was personal. I kept my promises that I made to my mother. I share all of this to echo something my dad has reminded me time and time again: "If it were easy, everyone would do it." The sleepless nights, the tears, the countless 2 am and 3 am calls to my dad when I was on the verge of giving up—all of it mattered. My parents stood beside me every step of the way, advocating for my needs and reminding me of my strength when I couldn't see it myself.

To know I've made my dad proud, despite everything that unfolded during this journey, is a feeling I can't put into words. And to know that my mom is smiling down from Heaven, watching her promise fulfilled—it means everything. Every obstacle, every setback, every ounce of doubt led to this moment. To hear people call me Doctor... makes every struggle worth it. Though my degree is still fresh, the road ahead feels wide open and filled with purpose. Rather than following the traditional path of academia, I made a conscious decision to put my knowledge and lived experiences to work in the community. I currently serve as a Case Manager at an organization committed to empowering Black and Brown youth on juvenile probation in historically under-resourced neighborhoods. Every day, I have the privilege of walking alongside young people as they navigate some of the toughest challenges life can throw at them, offering support, structure, and most importantly, belief in their potential.

In a short amount of time, my dedication and leadership have not gone unnoticed. I'm currently being considered for a promotion into a leadership role—a reflection of both the impact I've made and the trust my colleagues and supervisors have placed in me. This role would allow me to broaden my reach and help shape programming that addresses the root causes of youth involvement in the justice system.

Looking forward, my vision is even bigger. My ultimate goal is to establish a nonprofit organization that provides holistic support to justice-involved and at-risk youth. I don't plan to do this alone. I'm building this dream with a group of friends who, like me, have recently earned advanced degrees and are deeply committed to equity, healing, and generational change. Together, we aim to create safe spaces, opportunities, and resources for young people who have been counted out far too often. This is just the beginning, and I'm excited for what's to come.

To the brilliant Black women across the diaspora dreaming of a terminal degree—know this: you are your ancestors' wildest dreams made real. The journey may challenge your faith, your strength, and your peace, but remember, you were built for this. Every setback is preparing you for an incredible comeback. You carry the power of generations within you—resilient, brilliant, and unstoppable.

When you walk across that stage, you'll join the proud 2–3% of us who hold a Doctorate of Philosophy. And as my mother always reminded me: "They can take everything from you—but never your education." Keep going. Your crown is waiting.

"You are your ancestors' wildest dreams made real. The journey may challenge your faith, your strength, and your peace—but remember, you were built for this."

"Trust in the Lord with all your heart and lean not on your own understanding; in all your ways submit to him, and he will make your paths straight."

Proverbs 3:5-6

CHAPTER 7

DR. L'TOMAY VARLACK-BUTLER, MSW

Ain't I a Human? Survivor-Scholarship, Sacred Resistance, and the Making of a Woman Doctor. I found *The Woman Doctor* at a breaking point. After a committee member suddenly dropped off, my original defense date in November 2024 was delayed and nearly derailed. In that season of academic grief and disappointment, The Woman Doctor became a digital sanctuary. Her posts were encouraging and unapologetically powerful. They were balm to my soul. I downloaded them, read them in silence, and prayed when the noise got loud. They reminded me of who I am. When the institution tried to push my defense again, I pushed back and through. I defended on March 28, 2025. When it was over, my husband crowned me, literally with a crown on my head and a cognac, *The Woman Doctor* bag in my hand. This chapter is more than a reflection. It is my offering of gratitude. Because her words didn't just inspire me, they steadied me. They helped midwife my sacred becoming.

I wore an S on my chest, but not for "Supergirl." Mine stood for Secrets, Silence, and Solidarity. Solidarity with those who abused their power and forced my complicity. That's how my childhood began, not in innocence, but in encoded survival. My mother said I was different because I didn't like to play with other children. But it wasn't shyness. It was a shame. I didn't feel worthy of connection because of the trauma I carried, forced into hiding. But Saturday mornings gave me life with my mother blasting "Wake Up Everybody," the scent of cleaning products in the air, then we had the chance to watch our cartoons, eat breakfast, and later kung fu flicks with her imitating drunken monkey moves. Laughter lived there, if only briefly.

It was those memories that kept me as I experienced the intrusive ones, where the babysitter invaded my body at night. So the one place that I found safety was in school. It outweighed what took place at night, where my body became a battleground that I could not name. And so I buried my voice. School became a complicated sanctuary. I was paddled in front of the class in fourth grade for blurting out the response. I only did so because my arm was tired from holding it up, and at the time, I didn't have a name for why the only Black girl in the class was over-looked. Even after answering the question correctly, I was punished, which only made me stand in solidarity with the adults in power who taught me to remain silent. In fifth grade, I tried to speak about the harm happening at home. I was told that what happens at home stays at home. That, too,

became another layer of my silence. It was another lesson that taught me to stand in solidarity with those who keep secrets. But none of that prevented me from excelling in school. So, I excelled. I was an A student and even beat out 8th graders in the spelling bee, despite being in 5th grade. The false narratives I heard were that my good deeds weren't good enough, as I kept getting punished. I wrote stories that lit up classrooms, but they also got me expelled. By seventh grade, my writing, my imagination, and my voice, once praised, were deemed dangerous. A white teacher said she was afraid of me. My mother didn't know what to do. She enrolled me in public school, and the shift was seismic. I went from uniform to scrutiny, from brilliance to body conscious. Being expelled impacted me. One day after school, three teenage boys who went to my new public school waited for me in my building and dragged me to the roof and tried to assault me sexually. Although I felt worthless, dirty, and undeserving, the one thing I knew was that I had my brain and believed that I would get away from the things that haunted me daily.

So I graduated from public school that same year, out of 8th grade, and applied to the prestigious Fiorello H. LaGuardia High School of Music and Performing Arts as a vocal major. I held onto my voice through song, although I lived in silence from the secrets that I held in solidarity with the ones who caused harm. I survived. I kept going. And yet, I dreamed myself out of the box of trauma I was trapped in and held onto my voice through song, even as silence held me hostage.

When it came to being a doctor, there wasn't a single, blinding moment. There was no single epiphany. It was gradual, like a reckoning, where encouragers would show up along the way and remind me who I am. A soft and steady reclaiming. Healing circles. Spiritual awakenings. Moments where I realized I am not alone. I am not worthless. When I was in undergrad, I only knew that I wanted to be a healer. And then I had a conversation with my English professor. He asked to speak to me after class because 20% of my grade was participation, but I barely contributed because trauma had a chokehold on me. He said that when I did speak, it was as if I was embarrassed to do so. However, he continued, saying that what I shared was always profound and insightful, and that I had a brilliant mind. He told me to dig deep and find out why I was embarrassed to speak up, because the class only benefited when I spoke. My desire to pursue more than an undergrad degree was slowly simmering.

That S on my chest could mean more. It could mean Speaker, Scholar, Seeker of truth. I wanted to give language to the unspeakable. To be the kind of researcher who listens. To study systems not from a distance, but from the wound. To create space where others like me might see themselves as whole. Becoming a doctor wasn't about titles. It was about freedom. I pursued this degree because I was tired of being spoken about, rather than being heard. My Indigenous and Black ancestry, the Blackfeet, the Cherokee, and the descendants of the diaspora called me to speak truth to institutions that tried to erase us. I needed to know how to liberate Black girls like me, survivors, disabled, and unseen, who belonged and were often excluded and made to feel unworthy. Undergrad and graduate school only told one side of the story. I wanted to honor my grandparents' resistance against cultural erasure and live out a scholarship where I could study the why of the harmful silence that persisted. My degree became a path to liberation, a radical act of truth-telling. A calling to breathe life into language and dismantle the colonial impact that had policed my body and brilliance. The colonial violence left an imprint on the psyche of humanity.

Restorative justice became my pathway, not because it was popular, but because it held ancestral roots. Roots that were being misappropriated. I wanted to bring a decolonial lens to tell the truth behind the abstraction. After I dropped out of high school, I experienced harm again, this time by a neighbor's boyfriend. I became a teenage mother and eventually found solace in my safe space: the place no one could take away, my love for learning, and my search for meaning. I went back to school and I earned my GED. Education, though bruised and battered, was still my compass. I didn't trust institutions, but I trusted learning. I returned not just to prove something, but to be something and do something, healed, whole. I trusted God with my story. Before entering the doctoral program, I had already begun walking the long, sacred path of justice work. I was not simply preparing for the degree, I was living the work. I served as a social worker, executive coach, and restorative equity educator, standing in the gap for those too often overlooked or silenced. As the Sage Waymaker at Worth Justice Inc., I nurtured healing-centered spaces for individuals and communities deeply impacted by systemic harm. My work spanned borders, combating violence against women and youth in Haiti, cultivating restorative practices with HIV-affected adolescents in Romania, and fostering inclusive pedagogy in South Africa.

In academia, I taught with purpose and presence, not performance. I served as a Kings-Chavez-Parks visiting professor and held faculty roles at institutions like Metropolitan College of New York, Vermont

Law & Graduate School, and the University of San Diego's Restorative Justice Certificate Program. I collaborated with DEI leaders, educators, and community visionaries to disrupt extractive models of education and promote equity-centered transformation.

I also founded Brand Me Beautiful®, a healing initiative designed to empower women, girls, and survivors to counter harmful narratives and reclaim their sacred self. The media took notice, Capital B News 1, Teen Vogue 2, and WPIX 3 uplifted my advocacy and the transformative power of healing circles. These weren't résumé lines; they were rituals of resistance. As a Futures Without Violence Survivor Leadership Fellow and a scholar trained in integrative trauma through the National Institute for Psychotherapies, I carried the stories and scars of my community into every room I entered. This work, lived, embodied, and ancestral, was my prelude to the Ph.D., and the very reason I chose to pursue it. The doctoral program presented new challenges, including institutional colonialism disguised as academic rigor and silencing presented as professionalism. As a graduate assistant and resident restorative justice practitioner at a predominantly white institution, I witnessed firsthand how senior practitioners weaponized power. My reflective questions were met with microaggressions, and even when harmed, I was told to "fix the problem" —a problem they refused to name, but I did and was erased because of it. I turned inward. I wrote.

I created JOY: Joy Operating In You, a journal that became my sanctuary. I documented harm, but I also documented resistance. I held myself accountable for truth-speaking. To hold space, even when space tried to erase me. A transformative moment was my JOY development. JOY (Justice Operating in You) did not begin as a methodological practice. It was born out of necessity. A sacred response to harm. A container for my rage, grief, clarity, and resistance. It was an ethical way for me to transform the harm experienced and not transmit it. When I first began documenting my process, my dissertation was titled The Weight of Whiteness. That title captured the heaviness I carried, the harm, the silence, the attempted erasure. But as I journeyed deeper, I recognized that while the title pointed outward, I also needed to look inward.

Through JOY, I began to see how systems of oppression weren't just around me; they had taken root within me, shaping how I moved, spoke, and sometimes stayed silent. Influenced by Marimba Ani's rhetorical ethic, Kuntz's exploration of parrhesia, and Song's work on truthspeaking, I realized that authenticity, spiritual accountability, and radical honesty weren't just scholarly concepts; they were lifelines. JOY demanded that I reckon not only with external violence but with the internalized colonial narratives I had unconsciously carried.

One journal entry read:

"How do I trace harm without bleeding on the page?"

Another:

"Today, I refuse to be their data point. I am the data. I am the story they fear."

JOY became a living methodology. Not just a journal, but a ritual, a return to self. It invited me to disrupt inherited silences, to dismantle the systems of oppression operating within, and to begin the long, sacred process of healing the harm life had inscribed in my body. It showed me that in becoming a beloved community, I first had to build that community within myself. JOY didn't just hold my reflections, it held me. It became the grounding from which I could build a methodology and an analytical tool that ethically guides and anchors my work in integrity. It is the sacred container for speaking and holding internal truths.

It is through JOY that a truth-realization emerged: lived experience is empirical evidence. I am the truth, the data, and what research cannot express. My breath, my body, my breakdowns and breakthroughs, all carried data too sacred for footnotes. JOY reminded me that healing is not anecdotal. That pain, when spoken with clarity and care, becomes its own citation. Through JOY, I wasn't just recording emotions, I was identifying patterns, confronting systems, and tracing harm with the precision of a scholar and the soul of a survivor.

A Transformative Moment in the Doctoral Journey

There was a night, really a moment, when the past came back, not as memory, but as activation. I use the word 'activation' intentionally because 'trigger' can reverberate with the trauma that can be carried in the body. I understand this as I have survived gun violence. It is why I choose to use a different word. Activation is a way to honor the shift from becoming reactive to being relational. Language, words, discourse, and the way we communicate can frame, inflame, kill, or heal. So I chose a language that reflects my decolonial, trauma-informed, and survivor-centered commitment to transforming the way I see. I don't see an emotional response as a breakdown; instead, I see it as an invitation to self, a pathway to deepen awareness, a reclaiming of sacredness, and collective healing. That night, I turned to my journal. I wrote with a feeling like a ton of bricks caved in on me. I began with the title and a short entry.

The night, suicide said hi. It was just a thought and then a gloomy feeling. I thought it (suicide) was gone for good. I was experiencing multiple moments on an almost daily basis that consisted of attempted spirit murder where racism, where whiteness, acted like a butcher viewing me as game to be carved up and served for their good. Me—the woman, mother, daughter, the person, the girl, a human was never a first, second, or third choice. I believe my Blackness showed up too real. They did see me, it was just the erasure, the violence of their words and actions was both unreal and devastating. But I chose myself, I saw myself. That entry wasn't the end. It was the beginning of a new kind of clarity. A spiritual mirror. A fierce refusal to forget who I am and what I carry. What followed wasn't just breathwork, prayer, or mindfulness. It was a memory. Clarity. A sacred reckoning.

I remembered the white woman who policed my voice in a so-called restorative space. She told me not to say the word harm because it "activated" her while refusing to acknowledge the harm she herself inflicted. She erased my labor. She withheld my pay. She empowered a male colleague to verbally attack me on her behalf while she stood by with pride.

This wasn't discomfort. It wasn't miscommunication. It was violence. Colonial. Calculated. Civil in tone, brutal in impact. There was nothing restorative about it. It was the performance of allyship weaponized against truth. I did everything I was supposed to do. I prayed. I meditated. I turned to somatic healing, to ancestral breathwork. But the most powerful breakthrough came not through those rituals alone, but through remembrance. And then came the profound words from students whose lives I had touched. One shared in class: "Professor Douglas, you have the mind of Malcolm X and the heart of Dr. Martin Luther King. Another student said, "And I love your teachable moments, you reframed when something out of pocket was shared."Their words became fuel. They reminded me that I was not the problem. I was the portal. The healing. The teacher. The sanctuary. The one who created space even while standing in the storm. That moment was raw, unvarnished, and undeniably real, now living inside my framework, my methodology, my mission. Because liberation work must hold space for the nights we almost didn't make it. It must carry the weight of our near-endings and transform them into thresholds. This is why I am unashamed of being a Survivor-Scholar.

I survived the weight of whiteness that tried to bury me in a grave of silence and despair. This is what it means to be activated into purpose, not despite harm, but in sacred defiance of it. It was a defining moment that made me deeply curious about the power of language and discourse. I began to examine how words, when unchecked, could either harm or heal. In that same season, I learned of the heartbreaking death by suicide of Dr. Candia-Bailey, former Vice President of Student Affairs. Her passing was not just a tragedy; it was a mirror held up to all of us. Dr. Bailey left behind a note that laid bare the weight of her pain. She shared the dehumanizing dialogue, microassaults, and microaggressions, each of them undeniably macro, that had chipped away at her spirit. Her soul had endured so much that it was murdered long before she died by suicide. Her absence made clear that holding degrees, possessing skills, or occupying high-ranking positions does not exempt anyone from pain or despair. If anything, it makes understanding even more essential. Speaking on issues like suicide without genuine comprehension risks deepening the hurt of those grieving and further stigmatizing those who suffer in silence. Our unexamined assumptions and biases can compel others to mask their struggles behind a facade of normalcy, leaving families to shroud their loss in shame, creating deeper divides of misunderstanding and hurt. This moment taught me the necessity of transformative discourse, not as performance, but as practice. A practice of deep listening, of courageous conversation, of radical empathy and healing. Because words have power, and as I was reminded, so do I. And so do you.

The Sacred Return to Solidarity with Self

We are longing for a sense of belonging when we have been Belonging the whole time.

Dr. April Baker-Bell 4 shows us that trying to fit in, to blend in, and becoming complicit in your erasure doesn't change by the way you speak. So I created and coined the term "Slanguistic Justice" in my work. Assimilation is real, and that is why JOY is needed. JOY (Justice Operating in You) was never just a journal. It was a sanctuary. A methodology. An analytical tool born from ceremony, ethics, reflection, survival, and truthtelling that I created not only to trace harm but to transmute it. It held my truths when the academy tried to polish them away. It reminded me that healing and scholarship could co-exist, not in conflict, but in covenant. JOY became a mirror, showing me when I was speaking from pain and when I was speaking from purpose. It kept me rooted as I analyzed language that tried to silence people like me. It ensured that I didn't contaminate the findings with old wounds and that I didn't let them re-open me. It was within this sacred, reflexive space that I birthed a new framework, not only for research but for liberation. I developed the framework HEAL Humanity Now, and at the nuanced core of this framework, healing begins when we begin—

Holding Space for Truth

Engaging the Inner Terrain

Activating Ancestral Memory

Liberating Language & Legacy

HEAL is not a checklist; it's a calling. A roadmap for others who are not just seeking degrees, but instead seeking transformation in themselves, in their communities, and in the oppressive systems they seek to disrupt. It applies across disciplines because while the institution wasn't designed for us, you were divinely designed for it. This is the work. This is the walk. And this is what it means to come full circle. I started with an S on my chest for Secrets, Silence, and Solidarity with survival. I end with an S that now stands for: Survivor-Scholar. Seer. Sister who strengthens Sisters. Storyteller. Sacred Self.

And to every aspiring doctor or emerging doctor: Wear your S however you need to. Just don't forget, it was never about being super. It was always about sovereignty and knowing who you are, set apart for a time such as this. My husband crowned me on the day I successfully defended my thesis. However, I realize I had already been chosen. Not by institutions, but by God, by the resilience, grit, and gifts of my ancestors, by survival itself. Becoming a doctor was not the culmination of my journey. It was my return. To self. To story. To sacred knowing. And to every woman doctor reading this, you are not behind. You are right on time. We belong. We have been belonging. Welcome home.

"

"We are longing for a sense of belonging when we have been Belonging the whole time."

"Now faith is the substance of things hoped for, the evidence of things not seen."

Hebrews 11:1

CHAPTER 8

DR. NICOLE LITTLEJOHN

 Growing up in what I would call the ghetto of NW Washington, DC, everything seemed difficult except for school. Living in a neighborhood where all you saw was addiction all around you, but you knew you didn't want that to be you, I told myself every day, "I have to get out, by any means necessary. School was always an outlet for me, and I always did well without even trying. As the second born of four children, it was hard to be seen, but I knew bringing home good grades would at least give me a moment where it was all about me, as my siblings weren't as good when it came to school. Too bad that it never lasted long enough. When I made the honor roll, won a competition, or received an award, the tiniest sliver of sunshine peeked from behind the clouds for just enough time for me to feel fulfilled momentarily. It was hard growing up with nothing you could really call your own. I shared everything…. a room, a bed, food, and most importantly, time and attention.

My parents were never married, so I very rarely saw my biological father, but I always felt like I needed his approval. Right before my high school graduation, I found out that my father was diagnosed with Multiple Sclerosis (MS). During his battle, all I wanted to do was make him happy. However, what I didn't know was that this need would stay with me forever.

Becoming a doctor was never on the list of to-dos; however, neither was going to the military, having children, or buying a home, but here I am. Getting my doctorate seemed so farfetched in the grand scheme of life that I still can't believe I have it. Once I finished undergrad, I vowed never to go back to school. That held true until I was no longer on active duty and found myself without a job, two young children, and lots of bills. One day, a friend told me that I could go back to school using my Government Issued (GI) benefits and receive a monthly stipend that would cover my monthly bills, as the kids would say," say less". I leaped at the opportunity to get my master's degree and earn some money. A couple of years later, I received a letter stating that I still had money left to be used, and because my children were not of age to use it, I decided to pursue my PhD. I had no clue what I would use this degree for; however, since I was not the one paying for it, why not? Little did I know this was the thing I had been searching for to feel COMPLETE!

To be honest, I never truly wanted to pursue a terminal degree; a terminal degree pursued me. Remember when I said school was the only thing that brought me recognition? It still holds true even as I became an adult. Once I was on my doctoral journey, my parents bragged about me to anyone they could, and that brought me so much joy. To hear them get excited about something I was doing, to see the smiles on their faces when they said my name and PhD in the same sentence, felt phenomenal. I knew this was something I had to do, not that I truly wanted it for myself. No real thought or effort was put into starting this degree. This was going to be one for "them" and not necessarily for "me". Every degree I have earned after my undergraduate degree has been for face time ONLY! I have always been an attention seeker. Therefore, this was no different. Needing and wanting are two completely different things. The process was painless and easy, which made starting it a breeze, but it was what happened after that that changed the trajectory of my life forever.

My time in the doctoral program was HARD to say the least! Everything was difficult, and I mean everything. It was a challenge, following a roadblock and an obstacle. Staying awake at night to research and write my dissertation. Sleep became something I craved, but no longer a priority. Trying to manage my time to make deadlines for chapters. Time management is crucial for staying on track when aiming to complete tasks within a specific timeframe, as it involves taking time off work to write chapters and transcribe feedback. At some point in the process, I had to make this sacrifice. I tried to stay present for my kids and everything they had going on. Being the custodial parent made it difficult, but not impossible. This was not a sacrifice I was willing to make. Showing up is essential, and my babies will always know that Momma was there and was the loudest one out there cheering me on. Trying to co-parent with a person you are trying to heal from. Take time (make time) to pour back into yourself. Working a full-time job.

Someone must bring home the bacon (as a single mom), and I was the only option. Being a good daughter, sister, partner, and friend. I wanted to make sure in my moments of downtime that I was present for my village the same way they were there for me, dealing with the death of my father. This moment in my life broke me more than I knew. I took weeks off after his funeral, tried to return, and had to take more time off. Once I found my footing, I started again. Give yourself grace when you experience something traumatic, like losing a parent. It is okay, and everything will be as it should. Learning how to navigate life without one of my biggest motivators. I have to say that even though I endured a lot of heartbreak, heartburn, and grief during my journey, I would not change it for anything. My journey made me!

My greatest motivators from start to finish were my parents, Tondalayo Clemencia and Jonathan Littlejohn (deceased), my children Danielle (18) and Nathan Joseph (15), my best friend Dedra Johnson, my significant other, one of my other doctoral sisters, Dr. Charmelle Ackins, and most of all, *The Woman Doctor*. Whenever I needed a pick-me-up, all of them were there to lend a hand in ways that I needed them specifically from them.

From a shoulder to cry on, a venting session, proofreading a chapter, taking my kids for a few hours so that I could just sleep uninterrupted, or a motivational quote to make you dig deep and keep going, my village was the bees knees!!! During this season, I had wins, but some moments could have taken me out. My wins were small but mighty. I made sure to reward myself after finishing every class, every chapter, and especially after the completion of my dissertation and my defense. That sense of relief when you are finally done is like nothing you have ever felt before, unless you have experienced having a child. It is pure bliss. No one can take those accomplishments from you. It is yours!

Pure grit and determination, not to quit, is the only thing that got me through. After my father passed away, I wanted to give up. I wanted to hide under a rock and do absolutely nothing. However, several things kept me on track. One, I never wanted my kids to see me quit. Setting an example for them meant everything to me. Failing is one thing, but quitting is another. Two, I know my father would have wanted me to finish, so giving up was no longer an option. Once I put myself in the right headspace, I persevered, gave myself grace, and finally finished. I am now a doctor of academia, holding a PhD in Business Administration with a specialization in Computer Information Security. I am currently a Project Manager in the Cyber division of the Federal government. My plan is to find a part-time teaching job online, teaching master level classes in Cyber, Information Security, or Information Assurance. I enjoy what I do, and I am excited to be able to use my degree to get ahead in my career field. My kids are thriving. My daughter just graduated from high school, class of 2025, and will be heading to McDaniel College in the fall to study Biomedical Science. My son will be a sophomore in high school. They both hold above a 3.5 GPA. I am a proud member of Alpha Lambda Psi Military Spouses Sorority Inc. While serving as the Dean of Pledges, I also have a position as the Director of Fundraising for the UNITY Thunder youth development program. Lastly, I recently started my non-profit organization "Littlejohn Legacy," which was created in my father's honor to provide scholarships to those who are suffering from or have a family member suffering from MS to pursue higher education. Since he was always one of my driving factors to continuing my education, I couldn't think of a better way for his legacy to live on. Let's just say I am booked and busy!

Some words of love, encouragement, etc, for aspiring doctors would be:

Only take from others what speaks to you.

Your journey is something to be celebrated.

Celebrate small victories.

Time Management is a must.

Do not let someone else's issues become yours.

Do it scared and afraid.

It will be tough, but you must be tougher.

Take breaks, Rome wasn't built in a day.

Finish strong!

"

"My wins were small but mighty."

"For God has not given us a spirit of fear, but of power and of love and of a sound mind."

2 Timothy 1:7

CHAPTER 9

DR. ANNETTA CLARK

My Life Motivated

My childhood was interesting, having been born in January 1974 in Alabama. Imagine being inside your mom's stomach and your so-called father riding alongside her on the street, laughing while she is walking in extremely hot weather to a prenatal appointment. He and his friend are in the car laughing. Who does that? Well, it happened while I was in her stomach. Oh, but it gets better, shortly, she goes into labor, and you would think one would be excited about the arrival of a newborn, no, not my father.

Instead, he drops her off at the hospital and leaves. What could be more important than bringing life into the world? By the time he returned to the hospital, I had made my arrival into the world and was already named. Do you know he had the audacity to have an attitude? Oh, I'm sorry, Sir. I wasn't aware that I was supposed to wait until you were done running your errands to make my entrance into the world. Life was challenging for my mother as she tried to navigate the role of a new mother with little to no help. My Great Aunts helped her the most, as my mom shared stories about them, but it just wasn't enough to keep her in Alabama. My maternal Grandmother had favorites with her children, and my mom was not one of them.

On one occasion, my grandmother took care of me while my mom was at work, and that was the last time. My Grandmother made sure I ate, but she never changed me, so when my mom arrived to pick me up, I was still in the same diaper I had on when she dropped me off. Livid would be an understatement. You would think that being cared for by my paternal grandmother would be better, but it's not. She was bad, if not worse, and although she was willing to take care of me more than the other grandmother, she still had her doubts that I was her granddaughter. Things get a bit interesting around 18 months of my life when my father goes to prison. He and my grandfather got into an argument, a gun was pulled, a tussle occurred, and the gun went off. I can't even imagine the level of guilt for accidentally shooting your father. He served Media, not much. By the time I was 3 years old, he was released. Someone after I started kindergarten, and I can remember my fifth birthday party with my big wheel. I thought that gift was everything. My mother moved into her place, and it seemed as if things were going well. Unfortunately, that was short-lived. She had a new boyfriend, and apparently, he didn't know my mom could fight. They get into an argument, and he hits her. Let's just say that was the last hit he got in.

The next thing I know, the ambulance shows up to cart him off, not her. Not understanding at the time what had transpired, what I did know was that she won that fight, and I was excited.

That was the last straw; feeling defeated and unsupported, she packed up all our belongings and moved over 3,000 miles away to California: no family, just her best friend, and her two kids. Who moves away from the only family you know with a six-year-old? Looking back, that had to be the scariest, boldest, and craziest decision she had ever made, but it was for the best. As you continue reading, you will see that it was well worth it, and she made the best of it. Starting first grade at a new school, not knowing one person, was as scary as you can imagine. Moving on to the second and third grade, I had the same teacher, and we didn't get along. She said I talk too much, and I said to myself that her head was bigger than her entire body. Saying that out loud would have gotten me slapped, so I kept my thoughts to myself. She did teach me how to write in cursive, and to this day, I always get compliments about my penmanship. Fourth grade was a breeze until a bunch of boys running during recess bumped me into a brick wall, busting my lip. This would introduce me to my first encounter with discrimination. When my mother took me to the local medical center, my mother's medical coverage at the time was through Medicaid. They did not want to stitch my lip; my mother had to complain, and finally, they agreed to do it. She was afraid it would leave permanent damage, causing my lip to hang and cover part of my teeth, even when I smile. We revisited this when I got older, and that's when she explained the discrimination was linked to her receiving public assistance and them trying to deny aid to me. Well, fifth grade was interesting, considering I was part of a pilot program where freshmen and sixth graders were being taught by the same teacher in the same class. Don't ask, it was weird, but the teacher was amazing. Mrs. C was the best; she made us all personalized pillowcases at the end of the year. It was summer, my last year in elementary. I got to see my father for the first Media since his release from prison. I am back in Alabama for the summer, standing at the bus stop with my mother. A man walks up and speaks to my mom and then to me. They share a few words, and then he walks off. Keep in mind, I haven't seen him since I was three, so I don't remember what he looks like at this point. When I asked my mom who that was, she said Your father. I was in disbelief! Really? No, how are you doing? What have you been up to? How's life treating you? Nothing? He had a little boy with him, and one could assume that was his son, but I didn't ask. I was taken aback by the encounter. Why had he not kept in contact? Why the cold shoulder treatment? And just like that, we were back in California, and I was so lucky to get Mrs. C again as my sixth-grade teacher. Had the opportunity to compete in the district spelling bee that year and was the class speaker for our promotion ceremony. I had the audience laughing because I finally got to talk about my second and third-grade teachers in that speech - it was the best moment ever!

Moved on to junior high, and still had the opportunity to be around most of my friends until the school thought they were going to get over on placing me in a class with special needs kids due to overcrowding. The school told my mother that some kids transferred into the school, and they needed to move some kids around because the classes were overcrowded. Let's just say she arrived at the school that morning, I was enrolled at a different junior high by that afternoon. Not you placing me in a special needs classroom due to overcrowding is unreal. Once again, I found myself back at a new school, not knowing one soul, but now, I am 13 years old, and my thoughts process and feelings about this were very different. But once again, eventually, I made new friends and overcame it. I met my best friend here, not knowing she would not be my best friend throughout life, but that's a different story for another chapter. Now life begins, it's high school. I care about everything, my hair, my nails, my clothes, and the one thing that should have been the least important is what people thought of me. I was teased growing up, called blacky, darky because of the tone of my skin. I was not any guy's first pick to dances, homecomings, or anything, but I was smart and had long hair, and those were my superpowers, well, at least in my head anyway. That was one way for me to keep my head and self-esteem up, but I had a little help along the way. There was this one kid in church who used to tease me, and I didn't realize he liked me. One of his friends told me, and the next thing I knew, we were an item, and I was at his band performances at one of the rival high schools in the area. Once again, I felt like life was good, and by the end of my freshman year, I tried out to be a cheerleader. Something that started as a joke landed me on the varsity team. I made up the routine as I went along, dancing to "It Takes Two" by Rob Base, but my ending is what stole the show. I did a drop, and I could see from the judges' faces that they were in awe of it.

It's summer, going into my sophomore year, and starting to feel the pressure of "the birds and bees" conversation. I knew he was ready, but I wasn't, and I felt guilty. I felt like I was holding him back, so instead of addressing it, I picked a fight, and we broke up. I thought it was better that way, he could be free to do what he wanted and I sell had my virginity, at least for the next two years anyway. High school was great; I have no regrets, but now it was time for adulthood, starting a new journey in college. I attended a local university, unlike several of my friends who went off to college. Unfortunately, at the time, my mother was dealing with some medical issues, and I did not feel comfortable leaving, as I am her only child. I majored in Criminal Justice, thinking that law school was next because I wanted to be a criminal lawyer. By the Media my junior year rolled around, I had a change of heart.

My interest in being a lawyer slowly faded. I continued with my same major, hoping to find something else in the field that would interest me. One day, I was at home doing some research, and the phone rang. The gentleman on the other end asked to speak to my mother. I responded, informing him she was not home, and if I could take a message for her. "Is this Anita?" he said. I replied, "Annetta". He then said, "This is your dad." There was a moment of silence because, now that I'm older, I can remember that summer encounter where he only said Hi and walked off. I replied, "She's not here, did want to leave her a message." His request was for her to call him back. Here I am again finding myself in disbelief because now this was opportunity number two for him to have a conversation with me, and he didn't. After telling my mother the news, she explained why he was calling. My father was court-ordered by the state of Alabama to pay child support, but when my mother left and came to California, he no longer had to pay. Upon arriving in California, she relied on public assistance until she could get on her feet. Well, the state of California wanted their money back, so they went aÕer my father, garnishing his whole tax refund. The first thing that came to mind is that your tax refund is more important than having a relationship with your daughter. At this point, I had no more energy to give him.

Now, here I am, a junior in college, and Greek life started to spark my interest. Walking around campus every day and seeing all the sorority was a beautiful thing. Later on, in the same year, I became a member of Zeta Phi Beta Sorority, Incorporated, the best decision ever! As time progressed, my mom's medical condition got worse to the point she was forced to have surgery. She was down for about two months, but it was the best decision for her. After that, I couldn't keep up with her. She was gone with her bestie almost every weekend, driving up the coast of California. Since I didn't get the experience of going away to college, I decided to visit another CSU campus just to get the away-from-home expertise, so I set my sights on a college in the San Francisco Bay Area. It was considered a commuter college, but I didn't care; my initial thought was that this would be a one-semester thing, and then I would return to my campus. Oh boy, how the tables turned once I arrived. I loved it! I loved it so much that I transferred and never returned to my original CSU campus. I was able to bring back my sorority on this campus, became a tour guide and speaker for incoming transfer students, and graduated, not knowing what was next for me in life. It was tough, just when I thought things were looking up, 9-11 hit, and it changed everything. The job market was bad, trying to travel was worse, and the times were unknown and scary. I was working for a retailer at the time, so I remained there, was promoted to management, and did that for a couple of years, realizing this was not for me. Looking over my transcript, I decided to go back to school, majoring in Sociology with an option in Social Services. As I was approaching the end of the first half of the year, I found out I was expecting.

Not a part of my plans at that moment, but I was of an age where I felt like, well, if not now, when? Starting my internship and my second trimester at the same time was interesting. I thought many times that I should stop and start this at a later time, but I was too vested, and I loved the internship I had started with the local social services agency. Imagine working one job 32 hours, another job 8 hours, carrying 12 units as a full-time student, and working a 15-hour-a-week internship, all while pregnant!!! Who does that? Yeah, that was me. I'm not sure what I was thinking, but I finished, and my grades suffered a little. Still, I waddled across that stage and had my baby girl a week and a half later. It was so worth it. Now two bachelor's degrees and a kid later, I sell felt like something else was missing. I got engaged when my daughter was one, landed a job at my internship later that year, and got married a year later. Sell feeling as if I had not accomplished anything, I entered into a master's program. What was I thinking trying to do school now with a two-and-a-half-year-old? It was challenging, but when we

hear people say it takes a village, it was that for me, wholeheartedly. Having landed this job, I finally felt like I was doing something that was career-worthy. Graduated with my master's and life was good, I was satisfied, or so I thought. A little over a year went by, and I was assisting a student with his application for public assistance. Yep, remember the story about the busted lip in the fourth grade and the first encounter with discrimination? I decided to pay it forward, and by this time, I was about five years in at the local social services agency. This student came in and stated he was homeless, living in his car, and needed assistance with food. I knew there were regulation around students applying, but I was hoping he would qualify. Well, he didn't. I tried everything, including enlisting help from my supervisor and manager, but we were unable to get him the assistance he needed. He thanked me, but left crying. I felt so defeated as if the system had failed him. So, every student applicant afterward, I started to pay close attention. Some didn't care, as they were so hungry that they would withdraw from all their classes to qualify for assistance.

If the purpose of the public assistance programs is to supplement, why are students feeling like they have to pick between being educated and having something to eat? This sent me on a different mission because now I wanted to study it, analyze it, and try to figure it out. I began researching doctoral programs, and I recall feeling like I was done; life was good. However, now, once again, I feel like something is missing. Little did I know that four months later, I would start a doctoral program that would change who I am.

I remember attending my first residency and being told not to expect my dissertation to change the world. I thought to myself, maybe not change the world, but I can at least get the conversation started. And that was key in finding a dissertation topic, writing about something I am passionate about. These policy regulation around students qualifying to receive public assistance seem counterproductive.

My classes continued, and my dissertation topic developed as I got closer to the prospectus stage of my doctoral journey. This was where things became a bit discouraging. I was in my last class before entering the dissertation cohort to begin writing. I was excited because I started this class thinking I was ready, title in hand, research methodology chosen, and ready to create this prospectus to move on to the next phase. I am going through the class and receiving feedback for each section of the prospectus we submit weekly. I am under the impression I am doing good; I didn't have reason to think otherwise. This class is 11 weeks; the professor waited until the end of week eight to tell me my topic would never make it past the prospectus stage. She was aware of my topic in week two. Why would anyone wait until the end of week eight to tell me that? I was taken aback and felt hopeless because I had worked so hard to get to that point, and couldn't believe she said that to me and waited so long to do so. I had to step away for a couple of days before responding, which gave me Time to consider the most strategic approach. And it hit me, keep it simplistic. I told her Thank you, I will keep that in mind. I passed her class and had a prospectus in hand for my committee's review. After some edits suggested by my committee, my topic, which wasn't supposed to make it past the prospectus stage, was approved by the program director. Oh, what a happy day that was! Now the real work began. I was instructed to start with chapter two, the literature review. I had a rough start; I was a month in and only had four pages, and was feeling a bit lost. By this time, I had completed three of the four required residencies, so I decided to do a writing-intensive for my last one. This is where my motivation and purpose shifted, and I met three incredible ladies who would profoundly impact my life on this Ph.D. journey.

24Fifty was our crew's name, a crazy story behind it, but we came, we conquered, and we left with a different mindset on how to approach finishing this dissertation. We kept in touch throughout the years, and finally, it was their time; they had made it to the finish line, the graduating Class of 2019. I was so happy for them and grateful for the Ome we shared, but I knew the road ahead would become lonely without them. The challenges I faced were already significant, as I spent a year and three months trying to get my proposal approved due to the numerous edits and the difficulty in finding a reasonable editor to do a good job. I was able to defend my proposal and receive approval to move on to the IRB process. Upon returning from their graduation and celebrating with the 24Fifty crew, I was informed my committee chair was taking leave, and I would have to locate a new chair. I knew I could not have any setbacks, so I requested my second committee member to become my chair and began the search for a second committee member. It was not long before my second committee member was acquired, and I was able to focus on the IRB application truly. It was long and tedious, but I was able to finish and receive conditional approval after submitting some additional paperwork that required signatures. Ran into some challenges with a couple of the institutions I was recruiting from, but I was finally able to get full IRB approval on January 31, 2020. I began to receive participants willing to interview and was able to complete two interviews before the world shut down and COVID took over. March 10, 2020, will forever be sketched into my memory bank; life as we knew it was gone, and no one knew what was in store.

Now I have a different issue, I need a minimum of twelve participants. I'm now in a space where the participants I'm looking for have to do their job virtually, and they don't have time to entertain an interview with me. What am I going to do? I called my chair and we brainstormed and came up with a plan to go back to the IRB to adjust how I can get participants using social media platforms. It seemed like forever, but really, they got back to me in three days and approved the suggested adjustments. I utilized my social media platforms to schedule an additional seven interviews.

Then I was stuck; three weeks had gone by, and I had only completed nine interviews, leaving me three more to go. Using every connection I had, I secured six more interviews, bringing my total to 16 by June 22, 2020, amid the COVID-19 pandemic. Collecting data during this very unusual time is not for the weak! I took the enΘre summer to analyze, code, and write chapters four and five. On September 20, 2020, I submitted my first draft of my entire dissertation, and the last leg of this journey began. I had to get a new editor based on the feedback from the URR. Finally, just when I think everything is going well, I'm confronted with more challenges. I had been dealing with fibroids over the years, and at the most inopportune time, I had to have surgery to remove them, in addition to removing a hernia; this was a lot to deal with. I had the myomectomy on March 5, 2021, which had me down for three weeks. I defended my dissertation on April 8, 2021, and I had a hernia removed on April 13, 2021, which had me down for 5 weeks. By the time I returned to work, my Ph.D. was conferred on May 16, 2021, with the title, *The Supplemental Nutrition Assistance Program Work Policy and Its Influence on College Academic Success.* On July 31, 2021, I participated in a virtual graduation and was able to celebrate in person with all my family and friends on August 7, 2021. It wasn't until June 25, 2022, that I was able to cross the stage and be hooded as Dr. Annetta Ann Clark, Ph.D., in Public Policy and Administration from Walden University.

Even with all the challenges I have faced in life, those same challenges have motivated me to reach this point. I made an effort not to let what has happened to me define who I am or control the narrative of what I want to do. Having met the 24Fifty crew was a huge part of how I made it to the finish line. Even after they graduated, they continued to keep in touch, answering all my questions and helping me remain determined to complete my goal. My family and friends were understanding and flexible with me, supporting me when I felt I was at my lowest and could no longer continue, which made a huge difference during this journey. Since graduating, I was promoted to management within the social services agency and then transitioned to the training department. I am currently applying and looking forward to eventually transitioning to higher education to teach in my retirement years. Not only to pour into others what was poured into me, but also to help others realize their potential and the goals they can accomplish at any age. I recently witnessed two of my friends graduate with their doctoral degrees, one in the class of 2024, the other in the class of 2025. I saw their struggle and frustration, and I was grateful to be on this journey with them, offering encouragement and letting them know to keep going. Knowledge is power, and you are never too old to be educated. Remember, I started this journey wanting a JD, and now I have received a Ph.D.

"

"Knowledge is power, and you are never too old to be educated."

"God is within her, she will not fall;
God will help her at break of day."

Psalm 46:5

CHAPTER 10

REV. NICOLE D. HAWKINS, PH.D.

I grew up in a deeply community-oriented environment, where faith, education, and service were the core of our daily lives. I was raised to believe that leadership wasn't about titles, but about lifting others up and standing for something greater than yourself. Books, church, and community events shaped my imagination early on, and I always felt called to lead and to teach.

It wasn't a moment of certainty as much as a growing conviction. I knew that I wanted to be a lifelong learner, and that I had something valuable to contribute to how people lead and learn. When I realized how few Black women I saw with "Dr." before their names—especially in leadership and theological education—I knew I wanted to be one of them.

To me, pursuing a Ph.D. wasn't just about academic achievement—it was a commitment to impact. I wanted the tools, credentials, and research grounding to effect real change in education, ministry, and leadership development. It was also about legacy. I wanted to create pathways for others, especially women of color, to step into spaces where their voices are often underrepresented or undervalued.

Before starting my doctorate, I worked in a range of leadership roles across the public and private sectors, including nonprofits and higher education. I saw firsthand how policy, power, and leadership intersect—and how leadership development often lacked the ethical, inclusive, and human-centered grounding it needed. I pursued the doctorate to bring all these lived experiences into conversation with academic theory, research, and praxis.

There were plenty of challenges—balancing work, ministry, family, and study. I lost my full-time job, which ended up freeing my capacity to finish the degree in four years. Sometimes I doubted whether I belonged in the academy at all. But I leaned into community, prayer, mentors, and moments of rest. I also gave myself grace. I learned to trust the process, and more importantly, to trust myself. One day, one page, one prayer at a time.

I was motivated by every student I've mentored, every woman who thought it was too late, and every ancestor whose sacrifice made my journey possible. I carried their names in my heart. My family and my faith were my foundation. And every time I walked into a room and didn't see someone who looked like me, I remembered why I started.

Beyond the degree itself, one of my biggest wins was staying true to my voice. I was able to do meaningful research that reflects both scholarship and soul. I was also able to connect my academic work to real-world leadership and ministry, bridging the gap between theory and practice in ways that matter.

A fierce sense of purpose. I knew that this wasn't just about me—it was about who I represent, who's watching, and who's coming behind me. And honestly, it was also tenacity. I refused to quit. Even on the hardest days, I reminded myself:

"You were called to this."

Today, I serve as a faculty member, executive leadership coach, and speaker. I support institutions in building inclusive teaching cultures, mentor aspiring scholars, and advise faith and community leaders. I remain active in research, and I continue to walk in both academic and spiritual leadership spaces—doing work that equips others to lead with integrity.

To every aspiring doctor: You are worthy. You belong. The path may be long, but it's not impossible. Let your "why" guide you. Ask for help when you need it. Protect your peace and your vision. And know that finishing isn't just about the letters behind your name—it's about who you become in the process. You are writing more than a dissertation; you are writing history. Keep going.

"

"You are worthy. You belong.
The path may be long, but it's not
impossible."

"Peace I leave with you; my peace I give you… Do not let your hearts be troubled and do not be afraid."

John 14:27

CHAPTER 11

DR. ANESHA FULLER

 I considered my childhood to be a mixture of both God's grace and divine intervention in his plan. I had a childhood that was rough, as I migrated to the United States at the age of 1. I migrated with my dad and his family, and we absolutely left Jamaica with nothing to come to America, and rebuild our lives. Having come from a West Indian Background where Education is not free, my childhood was spent with education being my first and foremost priority, mixed in with a little bit of American culture as well.

I was always pushed to be actively involved in everything. Growing up, I was in the church children's choir. I was in every school play; I played the violin. I went to a Gifted and Talented program in JHS, and the list can go on and on. I was directed from an early age to be an overachiever and always go for the Gold. I developed the heart of a champion at an early age.

I can keenly remember when I was at my Master's Degree graduation from Touro College, and I saw all my professors and other impactful individuals sitting on the stage. I can keenly remember whispering to my friend who was graduating as well, "I want to be just like them". I said it, and then I eventually did it.

I decided to become a doctor because I wanted to become a College Professor. I knew that to be a college professor, you must have a Doctoral degree, especially in the subject areas that I wanted to teach.

The work or the process leading up to me pursuing my degree, as I was in a master's program for School Leadership, and I had just recently begun working at the New York City Department of Education. I was told by a co-worker that you need a certain number of years before you can be an administrator. I thought to myself in the meantime, while I acclimate to my year, let me pursue my terminal degree, and I can revisit my master's later, because I really wanted to be a college professor at night.

During my doctoral program, I found the core classes to be doable as the school prepared me for what to expect. However, my major challenge was with the dissertation. I had gotten into an argument with my Mentor, and it was awful. However, it ended up working out for me because we understood each other more and what works for us. I had a lot of times when I had to rewrite my paper because I wasn't writing it correctly, and I had to start over again. I can honestly say that I learned a lot from my challenges.

Some of the things that I learned were patience, taking my time, and strengthening my writing skills.

My motivation stemmed from a desire to see myself achieve my dream and reach the top. I am the type of person who describes myself as a Go-Getter. Nothing is impossible, and I can do anything that I set out to do. I also develop a strategy that I would work on ahead of time. Every time I got through one milestone, I was prepared for the next one.

My wins were that I was able to finish my doctoral program in three years. Some of the different individuals have taken four or more to finish. I was happy that I set a goal of the time that I wanted to finish, and I stuck with it and finished ON TIME.

I have always been very big on starting what I finish, no matter what the situation or scenario presents. I already knew I invested so much time and energy, and I also knew what I wanted. I started to follow a lot of individuals I saw on social media who obtained their degrees, and I used them as motivation. I knew if I could get across the finish line, the world would be mine for the taking.

I am currently teaching at an HS as a social studies teacher, and I am teaching in the evening at two of NYC colleges' undergraduate English courses. I recently went back to school for my master's degree in School Leadership and will be finished in May of 2022, moving towards pursuing a school leadership position.

To all my future aspiring doctors, NEVER and I mean NEVER give up. I was totally discouraged so many times throughout this journey. I was receiving discouragement from every possible area and person, and STILL, I NEVER gave up. The road may be rocky, but remember:

"

"The race is not for the swift, but for those who can endure."

"Do not grieve, for the joy of the Lord is your strength."

Nehemiah 8:10

CHAPTER 12

DR. DE`ANNA BOND, PHD

Dr. De`Anna Bond, the "Social Emotional Doctor," with over 20+ years of experience in the public sector (education, non-profits, mental health, and counseling). I have a PhD in Psychology from Capella University, M.A. in Counseling Psychology from Rosemont College, Education certification in School Guidance, and a B.A. in Psychology from Temple University. Over the years, I have been able to maximize my degrees to serve as a counseling professional, mental health provider, program developer, director, strategist, and technical assistance consultant. I have dedicated my career as an emotional intelligence (EI) consultant to enhancing the lives of others by building school teams and communities through education, advocacy, and mental health services/resources, social emotional learning research and programming, and raising awareness of personal wellness.

Reflecting on my childhood, I owe my village of family, loved ones, and community members for the major roles they have played in my upbringing and the things that I value. At a very young age, my mother also raised us to be strong, independent, and self-determined black women. She encouraged us to always pursue all the things we desired. We were exposed to different cultures, religions, history, the arts, community engagement, and volunteering. Even as a child, my education, getting good grades, and being the best that I could be were my goals. I was so hard on myself, and I never wanted to disappoint my parents or family. I understood that to get far in life, I had to pursue a college degree and get into places that allowed me to grow and show off my skills and talents.

Growing up, I always wanted to help and care for people. Early on in my undergraduate studies,

I took a Psychology course, and I was amazed how not only could I help people physically, but I could also help them mentally. I wanted to explore and understand the human mind and how our environments can mold us into the people that we are today. My classes were intriguing, challenged my thought processes, and most importantly, made me realize that in our black communities, there were no psychologists who looked like me. I knew then that it was my calling to pursue this as a career. I also understood that studying this major and working in this field would require me to get the highest degree possible.

While in my doctoral program, I spent a great deal of time traveling long distances for work, and this required many sacrifices. Oftentimes, that meant not spending time with my family, friends,

or loved ones. Working full-time and trying to obtain this degree took a toll on me mentally, physically, and emotionally. Life has a way of spinning you in ways that force you to self-reflect on the things that are most important. I would need to make major life decisions. Prioritizing my health was a struggle for me because my purpose has always been to serve and help others.

My significant life partner and I have always been great support systems for one another. He and I continuously encourage one another to make the necessary health/lifestyle changes,

pursue different career opportunities, as well as complete our terminal degrees. In addition, the support from my family, friends, and community has and continues to be rewarding and inspiring. I am extremely grateful to have all of them in my life.

In addition, identifying and securing a district/school for my doctoral research was very difficult and stressful. There were school leaders who were eager to have me speak with their students,

while others were reluctant to agree to my research. It was frustrating to have to wait for a school leader to trust me to come into their school environment and learn more about their students' experience with learning and using social-emotional skills. At times, I was unsure if I should have gone the route of researching schools and youth. Especially when some of the professionals who could benefit from this information second-guessed the purpose of my research. However, I was determined to have student voices heard and continued to use the work that I have also done in schools to advocate for them and explain their perspectives in a school environment.

I have had the opportunity to explore a different level of education and how my own research could inform the field of education and psychology. I realized that the social emotional learning (SEL) skills that I was teaching my young people, the adults in my professional circle needed to learn ways to use these skills as well. I began to look deep into myself and learn to leverage my own emotional intelligence (EI) skills. I learned to become more self-aware and made sure that I celebrated my wins, big and small. My passion, drive, and desire to want the best life motivates me to step out of my comfort zone and face fear and anxiety head-on. It has been using "EI" skills that I was able to successfully complete my own terminal degree, start businesses, get job promotions, build stronger business relationships and teams, and make better life/ career decisions. I am more self-aware of my strengths, recognize my areas of growth, and how to self-

Regulate my emotions during challenging times.

My company, Bond Consulting Group, LLC, is dedicated to offering high-quality services through the facilitation of Emotional Intelligence (EI) professional development training and consultations to educators, leaders, and organizational teams. As well as group coaching for entrepreneurs/business owners to address the psychological aspects of the business/work environment as it pertains to emotional intelligence development/social emotional learning, business advancement, personal and professional well-being. My e-course platform has helped

Individuals obtain advanced degrees, career advancement, and leadership opportunities.

Since receiving my degree, I have connected with so many wonderful women and men doctors in various industries. I have been coached and mentored by some of the best life coaches and psychologists. I have managed to build my network on multiple levels and through different social platforms such as *The Woman Doctor*. The Black Doctoral Network allowed me to present my research as well as be featured on their podcast series.

It has been so rewarding to speak on panels and local podcast shows, write and be featured in books, and connect with environments that can help me evolve. Increasing the number of black doctors in any field of study challenges the status quo. I challenge us all to not only be role models models, mentors, teachers/professors, coaches, and consultants to other doctoral students, but to continue to build communities and create network spaces for us to see and acknowledge one

Another as we change our history forever.

-Dr. Bond

"

"Life has a way of spinning you in ways that force you to self-reflect on the things that are most important."

"Fear not, for I am with you; be not dismayed, for I am your God. I will strengthen you, I will help you, I will uphold you with my righteous right hand."

Isaiah 41:10

CHAPTER 13

DR. SHOJI MALONE

 I was born and raised in Milwaukee, Wisconsin, to wonderful parents. They worked very hard to ensure that I had the best opportunities that life had to offer. They also ensured that I knew that God made me a powerful, intelligent, strong, and worthy person. With all of this in mind, my education was a priority. So, when I turned four, they naturally enrolled me in what was considered one of the best private preschool programs in the city. This school was in

Shorewood, and so demographically it was no surprise that I was the only black student in my class, and one of about five black students in the entire school. At this school, I remember attending field trips to the library, attending mass, and being invited to birthday parties. At that time, my very best friend had a birthday party at her house. Her family's home was close enough to Lake Michigan that you could see the water from one of their balconies. I walked into her house for the party, and when I walked in, it was the largest house that I had ever been in. It was like a museum. They had two playrooms for the kids and a nanny who was playing with us during the party. I had the best time in my 4-year-old life. When I got home, after my dad picked me up, I rushed to my mom with excitement to tell her what a wonderful time I had at the party. During that conversation, I asked my mom if we could get a house like my friend's home by the lake with the blue water, if I could have a playroom, and if I could get my hair cut in a bowl hair style like my friends. My mother immediately sat me down, and I will never forget her words. She said, "Your water is not going to be blue like the lake;

it's muddy. And we don't have a white picket fence around our house. But where you live, it's just as good as anywhere else. No, you will not get a haircut like them, your hair is nappy and it's beautiful. You are your mommy's African princess, and you are great just the way you are." That 5-minute conversation changed my life. I became acutely aware that I was different from my classmates; I was black. And my parents made sure that I was fortified in my identity as a black child. They bought me books with black characters. The art around my house featured black people only. I began African dance. The sounds of Frankly Beverly and Mase, Gladys Knight and the Pips, and many other legends filled my house.

Religion and spirituality were a large part of my life. I didn't know that the first two pages of my dissertation introduction would be based on my mom's Saturday night and Sunday morning ritual. My home church was a predominantly African American church. It was non-denominational, and my pastor was a woman. My childhood church gave me my first chance at public speaking, dancing, singing, reading scripture, and I even wrote poems and mini "blog" posts that would be printed and published in the weekly bulletin. Those people supported and fortified me. I didn't know then that everything I was observing would be the backdrop to what I would write about in my dissertation. I didn't know that the context of where I was being groomed spiritually would benefit me so much later in life. The church was my introduction to black women in leadership. After all, my pastor was "Rev. Dr." I didn't know exactly what that meant at the time. But I knew it was important. And people respected her. The second was in the elementary school I transferred to.

The next school year, I went into K-5 at a primarily black Christian charter school. There, I was met with a completely different experience that changed my life. This school had an all black staff. The principal was black, the teachers were black, the founder was black, and the lunch staff was black. And the student body was almost entirely black. I went from being 1/5 to my entire class looking like me. We didn't have mass, we had praise and worship that was very similar to what I heard at my church on Sundays. They gave us opportunities to sing, and there was a tambourine section. I excelled there. I had the opportunity to go on travel field trips to Baltimore to study Ichthyology, they took us to museums in Chicago, trips to Disney in Florida, spelunking in Colorado, and to the Grand Canyon. In addition, they emphasized science and math. I excelled at this school, so much so that I skipped the fifth grade. Because this school placed such an emphasis on science and math, I thought that I would become a pediatrician. My parents began talking to me about college in Elementary school, and my school talked a lot about college, so there was no doubt that I was going, and I was going to be a pediatrician. Plus, my pediatrician was black and I loved her. She was the epitome of everything I wanted to be. She was kind, very intelligent, good with words, humble, and honest. She was also the best at her job.

Between my pediatrician's example and the example of my school administrators, I was certain I wanted to be a pediatrician. Knowing my interests, my mother began to find programs that would help me in my journey to getting into college. So between middle school and high school, I participated in countless summer programs, year-long programs, weeklong programs, etc., dedicated to science and math. She found university students to tutor me in those areas, and sometimes those tutors would become like family. She would make them food, and she was almost like their mom while they were in school, far away from their families. As I write, I am thinking about how much my mother sacrificed to do this for me. She became a single mom when I was 11 years old, because my father passed away. She did all of these things while grieving and working multiple jobs. I'm more grateful now than I have ever been. Anyway, in addition to science and math, she knew I was interested in literature. I loved black history and learning about the past. I liked to write. So she found resources for me to be trained in those areas as well. She made sure that my work ethic was top tier, and she never accepted anything but my best efforts. She made sure that I knew that I could accomplish anything I wanted if I worked hard enough. And she expected me to do my best and show up as my best always.

By the time I got to high school, her main goal was to send me to college. And I was very excited about college, shows like College Hill were on TV, and Laguna Beach, Gossip Girl, and The Parkers. And I loved watching reruns of Sister Sister, especially those episodes where Tia and Tamera were in college. College seemed fun to me. But I also knew it was a means for me to gain independence and the way for me to make a significant amount of money (so I thought). From freshman year to senior year, I participated in all kinds of extra-curricular activities, and a part-time job, all while completing the Full IB program at school. I developed a group of friends who were also mission-minded and were focused on getting into college. So we formed study groups to study for the ACT. We met at each other's houses, parents would provide snacks, and we would get to work. I went on a college tour where I was exposed to IV league schools as well as HBCUs and other PWIs. Through high school, I was still interested in science, but around the summer before my senior year, I was introduced to the term publicist or public relations and marketing. So I was going back and forth between being a pediatrician and a marketing director. At the time, I wanted to go to Spelman, so I did everything I could to ensure that I was going. By the end of my senior year, I was so tired. I had gotten my acceptance letters and decided that Marquette was for me. And once I entered my summer program at Marquette, I was back to my original idea: I wanted to be a pediatrician. I completed my summer program and entered my freshman year of college. Before the school year began, a black woman administrator at Marquette brought me and a few of my friends into her office, and she made us sign over our egos. She said, " Sign it over. This means that you will do what these professors say. You will do what it takes to get this done. Even if it's inconvenient or you don't want to do it. Don't do anything illegal, immoral, or that will compromise your reputation. But do what you are assigned, handle your business. This is your life." My first semester, I took a calculus course, a theatre course, Chemistry, and Biology. I was over loaded and I don't know who told me to take those classes in the same semester, but it was horrible. And I performed horribly. And I hated the content. The classes were large and unbearable.

By the end of the semester, I was sure I didn't want to be premed any-more. During this process, a sense of failure came over me. I felt like I was letting my family down. To me, becoming a doctor was the most successful thing I could do. They made a lot of money, and I thought about how disappointed my mom would be if I didn't become a medical doctor. I felt defeated. I wasn't aware that you could become anoth-er kind of doctor. But I knew I could just quit. So I went to the Ca-reer Services office, completed one of those surveys about what career would best fit you. The survey indicated that I would be a good fit for a communications major. So the next semester, I began taking courses in communications.

By the time I was a sophomore, I was working an on-campus job and a job at a department store. But that wasn't sustainable. So I quit working at the department store, but my on-campus job didn't allow summer hours. So a friend of mine and I heard the university facilities were hiring student workers and paying $12 an hour. We went to the office, applied, and we both got the job. That summer, I worked as a janitor, cleaning out dorm rooms and getting them ready for students. It was cold, and we cleaned in some dorms that didn't have air conditioning. I didn't like the work, but I did get to meet some great people. In that process, I realized that I needed a plan for summer work, so I would have to do that job again. And that summer, George Zimmerman was on trial for murdering Trayvon Martin. At work, we all listened to the trial. George Zimmerman was not found guilty. I was outraged.

I didn't understand how that could happen. But a friend of mine, who was in law school, tweeted, "Just because the general public thinks a person is guilty, and evidence displays guilt, that doesn't automatically render a person guilty." So I became interested in the law. After all, if you can't be a doctor, the next best thing is a lawyer, right?

By the end of the summer, my hairdresser introduced me to my now long-time mentor. She went to Rufus King like I didn't; she got her

B.A. from Marquette, and she had recently gotten her law degree from Marquette. We were a match made in heaven. She hired me for my first internship at the law firm where she worked. I was a marketing intern, working on some legal research as well. This internship gave me experience in what it would be like to do legal work and work in marketing. I didn't necessarily like the work I did. But I knew it was valuable, and I made some really amazing connections there. This internship also allowed me to fulfill an internship requirement for the School of Communications.

I knew I needed a job for summer, so my then-boyfriend, now husband, told me about the McNair Scholars Program. He had participated in the program, and he told me that I could study anything I wanted and get paid for writing a large paper. It sounded like an excellent idea to me. Additionally, my mentor had also participated in the McNair program. So it was a win-win. My mentor introduced me to my research mentor, who guided me through two summers of undergraduate research. She was a black woman from DC. She was a professor in Marquette's law school, and she was also a history major. She was a perfect match for me. She guided me through the research process. And I learned so much. It was also inspiring to share what I was learning with my family and friends. It was amazing to see their faces light up when I was telling them something that they didn't know. So it wasn't just me learning; there were others learning as well. I loved talking about black women and legal history. Although I only conducted research in the summers, I spent the rest of my time still taking my communications and marketing classes, and interning in communications departments across the city. I never liked communication work, but these were jobs, and they allowed me to pay my rent and gain experience.

By my senior year, I had presented my research so many times, and I was deciding if I wanted to pursue a PhD. The problem was that professors who had PhDs and people who worked at universities always complained about how horrible their pay was. And, again, I was going to get the degree to make my family proud and to be able to take care of myself, my future family, and my mom, of course. How would I do that if I spent all those years in school with no income guarantees? I loved history, and I loved studying black legal history. But what would I do? I learned that I could apply for a PhD and a JD program at the same time. Some schools had joint programs. It was perfect.

My final semester, I was charged with completing my coursework in communications, applying to grad school, finding a job for the time before I would get into grad school, working on my internship, and taking the GRE. It was one heck of a semester. I applied to grad schools only because I didn't want to take the GRE and LSAT. I submitted 10 grad school applications. And got accepted into two schools, both in the DMV area.

When I got the news of my acceptance, I was actually at my corporate job, bored, thinking of a master plan to get out of working that day. I was ecstatic. University of Maryland, College Park. Wanted to fly me out to College Park to visit the campus and go through some interviews. I went, met the other PhD students, talked to faculty, met my soon-to-be advisor, and learned that the school was offering me a fully funded 5-year McNair post-baccalureate fellowship at the University of Maryland, College Park in the American Studies program. I wasn't 100% sure what American Studies was at the time, but I knew that the scholarship they produced was interdisciplinary, and that's what I needed. It was a miracle. I didn't have a master's degree, and they accepted me to the program based on my two-year McNair summer research paper. From that day forward, I knew I was going to become a doctor, just not an MD, a PHD.

I finished working my corporate job, moved to Maryland in August, and started my journey. I was 22 years old, in a PhD program. The transition was hard. It was overwhelming. Maryland was new, different, and expensive to live in. I felt like I was behind. When I entered my first class, I felt so out of place. The impostor syndrome set in, and I didn't know what to do. In my class, my colleagues were all older than me, they were clear about what kind of scholarship they wanted to work on, and I felt so behind. Other students would use words like conviviality, vis-à-vis, and writ large. I felt so out of place. I felt like I didn't deserve to be there. I couldn't get my bearings. I never understood the readings, I had never heard of black feminism, and I was always behind in reading. I think I was reading something close to a book a week per class. I was tired. I was depressed. My life changed so much. In my mind, I went from being an overachiever to an underachiever. I didn't have my family or friends to lean on. It was so unfamiliar. And I cried almost every day. By boyfriend and now husband, I found a church home for us to attend, I got a job, and I joined a chapter of my sorority. But things weren't necessarily looking brighter. I was just getting busier.

And I continued with the busy schedule just like I had done my entire life. I never took a break. I was taught to keep pushing, fighting, and working towards the goal. And I did that for the next several years. But I wasn't necessarily learning or sharpening my skills; I was learning to get by and just make it happen. By the end of my second year, I was teaching a section of American Studies 101, working a part-time job, and taking three classes. I was still depressed but functioning. So things were fine, right? WRONG! I had a small wedding ceremony at my church, my then-husband and I got an apartment, I had recently gotten myself an internship at a government agency, and I thought I was succeeding. Until I was fired from my government internship because they said I didn't write well. My husband was fired from his job the day before. It was such a difficult time. I called my advisor, who was a Black woman, and she had recently been appointed to the department chair position. She said, "Don't worry about it." And she began hiring me to drive her daughter to practices and meetings, so I could sit with the kids. She gave me an option for income. And then the semester started, my husband got a new job, and things were looking up, kind of. I was teaching two sections and working as the American Studies department ambassador.

My mind was all over the place. I was trying to get used to being a wife and living with a spouse, managing almost 40 students, and still taking a full course load. In addition, we decided to buy a townhouse and plan a wedding. It was a nightmare. On December 30th, we closed on our house. And moved on December 31st. I went to watch a night service at church, because I didn't know how to communicate that I was tired. And January 1st, I sat down and didn't want to get back up again. That moment, sitting in our brand new home and not being able to move, was the turning point. I was no longer functional and depressed; I was just depressed. I did teach a winter term course, from my bed with so little effort. And I had teaching obligations in the spring, but that's the only thing I did. I was always exhausted. If I didn't have to teach or go to church, I wouldn't get up. I was crying a lot, I was angry, and I just didn't know what to do. That semester, I was supposed to be working on my second benchmark. But I made no progress. Towards the middle of the semester, my advisor saw that something was wrong; she brought me into her office and told me to shut the door. She looked me dead in my eyes and said, "Take a break, I know where you are, and I've been there. I'm not going to let you fail. You are going to finish this program. But you can't finish it like this." She referred me to the counseling center. I had a session with a white, male therapist, which I was against, but he was the only person available. I went into his office skeptical. But once I stopped crying and talking in between crying long enough, he said some really powerful things. He acknowledged that I was doing and trying to conform to what everyone said I should be. Religious institutions were dictating my measurements of how good of a wife and Christian I was being, public intellectuals, old job supervisor, and random know-it-alls on the internet were telling me how I should think, and how horrible of a scholar I was. And I was just stuck in between it all. I was so lost. I couldn't find my voice. Everyone else's tone was much louder than my own voice. I couldn't run into busyness anymore. I had to stop and find a little piece of myself to hold on to.

I was so worried about what other people said I wasn't good at, or comparing myself to the people who sound intelligent. I had developed a writing anxiety, in addition to general anxiety. But his advice was paramount. He said, "You don't have to be like anyone else, or think like anyone else, or operate like anyone else." He instructed me to look at his desk. When I looked, I saw papers everywhere, paperclips not attached to paper, pens all over, and folders and sticky notes lying around. He said, "This is my desk. I work here, and I'm very successful at my job. I very rarely miss deadlines. This works for me. A messy desk works for me. And I don't have to change the way I do because someone says I do. This is how I do it. And that's perfectly ok." Those words were so liberating to me. I always felt like I had to conform to what people said was the best way to do something. I never thought that my way was the best way for me. That was the beginning of my journey to healing and wholeness.

The next few years, up until this moment, have been spent on this journey. I applied for several opportunities, fellowships, conferences, and publications. I was getting several denials, and I got maybe three or four "yes's." What I learned is that what is for you is truly for you. At this point, I'm being called on for opportunities that I never would have thought about. I was sad with those denials, but now I'm much more prepared when a "yes" comes along. I know how to communicate my ideas better. I'm much more familiar with my voice. Additionally, I found several black women therapists to help me along the road. I ended up getting married and having a huge wedding that I attended while clinically depressed. I lost friends, I experienced hurt, and I gained new friends. And I'm still allowing God to build my tribe. I have learned the importance of community. And much of the reason that I have been able to finish is because of that community.

One of the greatest things I did was join a community in DC called SisterMentors. It's a community for girls and women who are pursuing higher education to get resources and guidance as they pursue higher education. SisterMentors has helped several women get their PhD. When I joined the community, I had completed my proposal, and I was at the beginning of the dissertation chapter writing. I was insecure about writing a dissertation about church women and hats, because it was unconventional and had never been done. I was also a part of the community that I was writing about, so I was nervous. Additionally, when church people that I encountered asked about what I was doing in school, I and I told them what I was writing about, I always got responses like "Oh, ok." Or smiles and nods. Even my own family members told me that I shouldn't be studying that and that I should study something else about black history and church people. It was as if people only wanted to know when I would graduate, and they never sought to understand what I was doing. It was annoying and discouraging. More often than not, people thought that I wasn't working. They would say, " So are you working tomorrow? Can you do XYZ for me?" As if writing a dissertation were subjective or not a "real" job. People's comments plagued me for a while, and joining this community and staying in therapy helped me to remember to drown out what everyone else thought.

Outside my relationship with Jesus, remembering that everyone's opinion doesn't matter is a major key. My work and scholarship are something that interests me and that I think is important. Furthermore, my committee thought it was important. Now, they did have differences of opinion about how the study could have been conducted, but they completely approved the project.

As I sit and reflect, I recognize that I was so beaten up by the graduate school/dissertation process. It often made me feel inadequate. I went into the program very ambigous, and I came out partly ambiguous. But the more I continue to press forward, I'm getting my stride back. One thing I learned is to work at my own pace and in my own way. The dissertation project is a defining moment in your life, but your successes and failures don't define you. You don't have to be like anyone else; the dissertation and your subsequent work should reflect your passion and love for your contributions to the scholastic world and community. It shouldn't just be what you think others want to hear or read. I didn't know who I was when I started; I didn't have language for what I wanted to do or who I wanted to be. But all along, I just wanted to tell the stories of everyday black women who decided to dedicate their lives to Jesus and build communities of faith.

Some of these stories had been told before, but many had not. And that's who I was focused on. Those people who literally build communities and culture but never make the newspaper. The ones that challenge the status quo and traverse political landscapes but never step foot into Congress. The ones who build movements, businesses, raise children, feed everyone, and sing hymns at 4 am, calling for God's mercy and praying for God's mercy and protection. The ones that never got to preach sermons or mount a pulpit because of their gender, but walked as living epistles. The ones whose voices were squelched by violence, racism, and sexism. Those women helped build this nation. And they are just as important as learning about Abraham Lincoln or anyone else in a history class. And that's it. That's what kept me going. I wanted to tell their stories, well, I wanted them to tell their own stories. I was just the vessel to disseminate them.

Through their narratives, I found language for who I am and what I do. I'm a storyteller, a collaborator, a womanist, a Believer in Jesus Christ, an encourager, a teacher, an interdisciplinary scholar, a humanities scholar with a love of black history and culture, a feeler, and a thinker. Now that my

dissertation, Rubies in Their Crowns: An Examination of African American Church Women and

Head Fashion" is finished. I am working as an African American Studies professor, and I work as a content consultant and researcher for museums and nonprofits.

I want to leave you with this. I learned that the words of Maya Angelou are true, particularly for black women PhDs, we "come as one, but stand as 10,000." Although we may look like one person standing at the podium giving a lecture, we have the strength of the Lord and our foremothers pushing us. We come from a relentless, creative, diligent, intelligent, and resilient people. The power that resides is a force to be reckoned with. But although you are powerful, you are still human. You need times of personal development, rest, and rejuvenation. You need time away to ask yourself the hard questions. You need people with whom you can be yourself. You need a safe space to cry. You need love. You need mindless activities, you need exercise. You need brunch with your girlfriends. As you continue through your PhD journey, know you deserve to be in those rooms; your voice is necessary. Your project is worthy and will contribute to knowledge production. If others don't believe, that just means your work isn't for them. And that's ok! You are going to finish. Cry it out. Take a 20-minute break and get back to it. You've got this! One thing I've had to do is affirm myself a lot. You can adopt the same affirmation: I'm worthy enough, I'm smart enough, I am enough, I am powerful, I can do this." We may never meet, but I'm in your corner. I'm cheering on every black woman chasing her dream.

We come from a relentless, creative, diligent, intelligent, and resilient people. The power that resides is a force to be reckoned with. But although you are powerful, you are still human."

"

" One day you'll look up and be reminded that your achievement is someone's dream."

"Let us not become weary in doing good, for at the proper time we will reap a harvest if we do not give up."

Galatians 6:9

CHAPTER 14

TIFFANY WELLS, PHD

As a child, one of my fondest memories is being called "poor little rich girl" by my grandfather. I never understood what it meant as a child, but as an adult, I realized the significant financial responsibility required to provide a comfortable lifestyle for myself and my children, and it became clear. I grew up in one of the most dangerous neighborhoods in Duval County. Although it was a very tight-knit neighborhood with generations of families, it wasn't uncommon to overhear about murders, arrests, and drugs. My grandparents had one of the most respected homes in the neighborhood. I recall people coming by to get sandwiches and other food around the house. I was my grandparents' most prized possession. My father was in prison, serving a 25-year mandatory sentence for multiple robberies. My mother, a recovering crack cocaine addict, was once known as very beautiful and the girlfriend of many major drug dealers in her younger years. She later reached sobriety, but that came at the cost of leaving me in the care of my grandparents.

I initially had dreams of being a Lawyer. As a child, I recall my grandparents having books custom-made for me, featuring characters with my name, and telling me I would be an attorney when I grew up. I knew I wanted to become a doctor after realizing the respect that came with the role. After receiving my master's, although I know I had essentially beaten the odds of so much stacked against my favor, being a teen mom at 15, having absent parents, and failed relationships. I knew I wanted to be unique; I knew that becoming a doctor would put me in the category of one of the most profound and brilliant thinkers. I knew this was something I could achieve.

There is an old saying that people ask you, " What do you do?" to determine the level of respect they are willing to give. Although skilled in my field, I was aware that certain opportunities were exclusive to terminal degree holders. I knew that to be top in my field, I had to do the things that others lacked the strength, motivation, or tenacity to endure and complete.

LIFE was challenging. I believe that during my doctoral journey, life was throwing everything at me. Marriage, career changes, academic hazing, ungovernable children, death, depression, pregnancy, infidelity, divorce, pre-foreclosure, illness. Murphy's Law says if it can go wrong, it will go wrong. I overcame it through consistency. I wasn't always motivated, but I was consistent. Social Media connected me to the most powerful women who had gone through the process, and they held me accountable. Did I mention Comprehensive Exams?

I think my biggest win was completing my program. This journey is truly the essence of marathon running. To be honest, I am the most non-athletic, unmotivated, and physically inactive person among all my family, friends, and co-workers. However, in that same token, marathon running and completion are about consistency. I wasn't always the fastest during this marathon, but my consistency kept me in the race.

It was understood that I was my ancestors' wildest dream. Understanding someone was a martyr for my success. Accountability partners, mentors from the Women Doc University. Writing my name down with Dr. in front of it.

I am currently in Florida. I am a program manager for the Centers for Disease Control in conjunction with one of the largest school districts in Florida. I provide surveillance and oversee program implementation for suicide prevention, sexual health, sexual education, and safe and supportive environments. I oversee a multimillion-dollar collaborative agreement and gain community support.

The best dissertation is a finished dissertation. One day, you'll look up and be reminded that your achievement is someone's dream. You will be in the 2% club. You just got to want it as bad as you need air to breathe.

"

"I wasn't always the fastest during this marathon, but my consistency kept me in the race."

"Blessed is the one who perseveres under trial because, having stood the test, that person will receive the crown of life that the Lord has promised to those who love him."

James 1:12

CHAPTER 15

DR. MARQUITA A. TAYLOR

I didn't pursue a doctorate for the title. I pursued it because something in me refused to settle for silence, for invisibility, for limits that were never mine to carry in the first place.

The journey to "Dr. Taylor" was both sacred and searing. I walked it while leading, while battling cancer, while healing, while lifting others, even as I was still learning to hold myself. As a Black woman in academic medicine and organizational leadership, I am often the only one who looks like me in the room. And when I am not the only one, I am still expected to *represent*, to *explain*, to *endure*.

My doctorate doesn't shield me from reality, but it gives me language, leverage, and a more profound sense of purpose. It gives me fire.

I earned my degree while demanding excellence, leading initiatives, and mentoring others who were navigating systems that hadn't yet made space for their brilliance. I was doing the work in my scholarship, and in my soul.

Most days I wore confidence like armor, afraid of letting anyone see the weight I was carrying. I never considered giving up, I thought of the little Black girls who were and would look up to me. I thought of the students who had never had a professor who looked like me. I thought of the communities I serve, of the stories, the data, the disparities that deserved a voice like mine. And I kept going.

I wasn't just earning a degree, I was breaking cycles. I was honoring my ancestors. I was creating new narratives for women who refuse to be boxed in.

There is something powerful about finishing what you start, even when the world is pulling at you from all directions. There's something divine about walking across a stage with a crown no one else can see but everyone *feels*. My doctorate isn't just a credential, it's a covenant, a commitment to speak truth, to challenge systems, to hold doors open for those still climbing.

When people say "Congratulations, Dr. Taylor," I smile, but what I feel is *clarity.* Clarity that I was called to this. That I am not here by accident or accommodation. That I earned every syllable of this title. With sacrifice. With sweat. With spirit.

So if you are somewhere in the middle of your doctoral journey, or still imagining whether it's possible for you, hear this:

It won't be easy. But it will be worth it.
It won't be linear. But it will be transformative.
You may question yourself. But that doesn't mean you're not meant to be here.

You are.
You always were.
Now, go claim your crown.
To God be the Glory,

-Dr. Taylor
Amen.

The Beauty of a Doctoral Degree: Praise and Worship

The Beauty of a Doctoral Degree: Motivation